INTRODUCING
ISSUES WITH
OPPOSING
VIEWPOINTS®

Teen Pregnancy

Other books in the Introducing Issues
with Opposing Viewpoints series:

Advertising
AIDS
Alcohol
Animal Rights
Civil Liberties
Cloning
The Death Penalty
Drug Abuse
Drunk Driving
Energy Alternatives
The Environment
Euthanasia
Gangs
Gay Marriage
Genetic Engineering
Global Warming
Gun Control
Islam
Military Draft
Obesity
Racism
Smoking
Terrorism
UFOs

INTRODUCING
ISSUES WITH
OPPOSING
VIEWPOINTS®

Teen Pregnancy

Emma Carlson Berne, *Book Editor*

Christine Nasso, *Publisher*
Elizabeth Des Chenes, *Managing Editor*

GREENHAVEN PRESS
An imprint of Thomson Gale, a part of The Thomson Corporation

THOMSON
™
GALE

Detroit • New York • San Francisco • New Haven, Conn. • Waterville, Maine • London

For more information, contact
Greenhaven Press
27500 Drake Rd.
Farmington Hills, MI 48331-3535
Or you can visit our Internet site at http://www.gale.com

LIBRARY OF CONGRESS CATALOGING-IN-PUBLICATION DATA

Teen pregnancy / Emma Carlson Berne, book editor.
   p. cm. — (Introducing issues with opposing viewpoints)
 Includes bibliographical references and index.
 ISBN-13: 978-0-7377-3625-0 (hardcover)
 ISBN-10: 0-7377-3625-9 (hardcover)
 1. Teenage pregnancy—United States. 2. Abortion—United States. I. Berne, Emma Carlson.
  HQ759.4.T4217 2006
  306.874'30973—dc22

                                           2006029461

Contents

Foreword

I ndulging in a wide spectrum of ideas, beliefs, and perspectives is a critical cornerstone of democracy. After all, it is often debates over differences of opinion, such as whether to legalize abortion, how to treat prisoners, or when to enact the death penalty, that shape our society and drive it forward. Such diversity of thought is frequently regarded as the hallmark of a healthy and civilized culture. As the Reverend Clifford Schutjer of the First Congregational Church in Mansfield, Ohio, declared in a 2001 sermon, "Surrounding oneself with only like-minded people, restricting what we listen to or read only to what we find agreeable is irresponsible. Refusing to entertain doubts once we make up our minds is a subtle but deadly form of arrogance." With this advice in mind, Introducing Issues with Opposing Viewpoints books aim to open readers' minds to the critically divergent views that comprise our world's most important debates.

Introducing Issues with Opposing Viewpoints simplifies for students the enormous and often overwhelming mass of material now available via print and electronic media. Collected in every volume is an array of opinions that captures the essence of a particular controversy or topic. Introducing Issues with Opposing Viewpoints books embody the spirit of nineteenth-century journalist Charles A. Dana's axiom: "Fight for your opinions, but do not believe that they contain the whole truth, or the only truth." Absorbing such contrasting opinions teaches students to analyze the strength of an argument and compare it to its opposition. From this process readers can inform and strengthen their own opinions, or be exposed to new information that will change their minds. Introducing Issues with Opposing Viewpoints is a mosaic of different voices. The authors are statesmen, pundits, academics, journalists, corporations, and ordinary people who have felt compelled to share their experiences and ideas in a public forum. Their words have been collected from newspapers, journals, books, speeches, interviews, and the Internet, the fastest growing body of opinionated material in the world.

Introducing Issues with Opposing Viewpoints shares many of the well-known features of its critically acclaimed parent series, Opposing Viewpoints. The articles are presented in a pro/con format, allowing readers to absorb divergent perspectives side by side. Active reading questions preface each viewpoint, requiring the student to approach the material thoughtfully and carefully. Useful charts, graphs, and cartoons supplement each article. A thorough introduction provides readers with crucial background on an issue. An annotated bibliography points the reader toward articles, books, and Web sites that contain additional information on the topic. An appendix of organizations to contact contains a wide variety of charities, nonprofit organizations, political groups, and private enterprises that each hold a position on the issue at hand. Finally, a comprehensive index allows readers to locate content quickly and efficiently.

Introducing Issues with Opposing Viewpoints is also significantly different from Opposing Viewpoints. As the series title implies, its presentation will help introduce students to the concept of opposing viewpoints, and learn to use this material to aid in critical writing and debate. The series' four-color, accessible format makes the books attractive and inviting to readers of all levels. In addition, each viewpoint has been carefully edited to maximize a reader's understanding of the content. Short but thorough viewpoints capture the essence of an argument. A substantial, thought-provoking essay question placed at the end of each viewpoint asks the student to further investigate the issues raised in the viewpoint, compare and contrast two authors' arguments, or consider how one might go about forming an opinion on the topic at hand. Each viewpoint contains sidebars that include at-a-glance information and handy statistics. A Facts About section located in the back of the book further supplies students with relevant facts and figures.

Following in the tradition of the Opposing Viewpoints series, Greenhaven Press continues to provide readers with invaluable exposure to the controversial issues that shape our world. As John Stuart Mill once wrote: "The only way in which a human being can make some approach to knowing the whole of a subject is by hearing what can be said about it by persons of every variety of opinion and studying all modes in which it can be looked at by every character of mind. No wise man ever acquired his wisdom in any mode but this." It is to this principle that Introducing Issues with Opposing Viewpoints books are dedicated.

Introduction

"Teenagers are not mature enough to know all the ramifications of what they're doing."
—Paul Coleman, psychologist and author of *The Complete Idiot's Guide to Intimacy*

"We should not underestimate young people's ability to see some of the complexities in a range of issues including sexual behavior."
—Robert Blum, professor of population and family health sciences, Johns Hopkins University

The United States has the highest teen pregnancy rate of any country in the industrialized world, including France, Germany, and Canada. Every year about 820,000 teens will become pregnant. Upon close inspection, the issue of teen pregnancy is in many ways about who is responsible for a teenager's body. Do parents hold the rights over their children's bodies and thus the responsibility for their actions? Or do teens have rights and responsibilities for their own bodies?

Though underage, teenagers are no longer children; they have adult bodies and adult feelings that often involve sex and pregnancy. Yet society has decreed that they need the protection and guidance of parents and guardians until they are eighteen. Parents also have a duty to teach and protect their children and to absorb the consequences of their actions. Many teenagers, however, especially older ones, are only a year or two away from legally being adults themselves. They make many important life decisions on their own and are deemed responsible enough to hold jobs, drive cars, and babysit. Thus, many mixed messages are sent about teens' responsibility, further complicating the issue when it comes to teen pregnancy.

Many parents and conservative political and social groups say that parents alone have the ultimate rights over, and responsibility for, their teenage children's bodies. Since a teenager is still a minor, parents have the undeniable right to be involved in all decisions in that teenager's life, especially those surrounding sex and pregnancy. But some institutions, such as schools, medical clinics, and nonprofit groups, offer services for pregnant teenagers and those who may become pregnant, without requiring permission from a parent. In doing so, these institutions violate parental rights, those who believe in ultimate parental rights say. Teenagers should not, in their opinion, be able to obtain an abortion without parental consent. Author Clarke D. Forsythe writes, "Minors are usually too immature to assess the safety of abortion clinics. . . . In addition, they need the guidance of parents to assess the risks of abortion . . . and parental notice is necessary to enable parents to care for their daughter afterward." Many parents argue that teenagers should also need parental permission to

A teenage girl and her father engage in a serious discussion. There is debate on how involved parents should be in their teens' lives.

obtain birth control or put a baby up for adoption—these decisions are too large for a teen to make alone.

In addition, parental rights groups and conservative political organizations argue that parents have the ultimate rights over their children's minds as well as their bodies. They therefore have the responsibility to control what their teenagers learn about sex and pregnancy. In their view, sexuality and pregnancy education are the domain of the family, not the government or the public schools. Topics such as contraception, sexually transmitted diseases, and pregnancy are intensely private. Opinions on how and what teenagers should know about sex are specific to each family. It is from this perspective that popular columnist Cal Thomas writes, "The government schools . . . aren't about to fix the problem [of teen pregnancy]. The responsibility to properly raise children belongs to parents. The state and interest groups have no right to develop the moral fiber of a child."

Many teen activists and liberal political and social groups believe just the opposite, however. They argue that even though teens are still minors, they have the right to be responsible for their own bodies and to control what they do with them. No matter what the decision—whether to have sex, use birth control, or abort a pregnancy—teens should be given all the options available and then be permitted to choose for themselves, with or without a parent's consent.

Moreover, these groups argue, nonparental figures such as doctors and clinics should have the right to interact with a pregnant teen without the involvement of her parents. Clinics should be permitted to give teens birth control if needed and provide pregnancy advice and counseling, even to provide abortions without a parent's permission. Some teenagers come from abusive homes or other dangerous situations where telling a parent about a pregnancy could put the teen at risk. In some cases, a teenager may need an emergency abortion to save her life, leaving no time to get a parent's permission. It is therefore a pregnant teen's safety and welfare that is important to those who would protect her ability to seek help without parental involvement.

Teen activists also argue that adolescents have the right to sex education so that they are capable of making responsible sexual decisions. In fact, withholding information about birth control, sexually transmitted diseases, or abortion, they claim, is dangerous and unfair. "Knowledge is power," writes author Dianne Rinehart, "and if we

Planned Parenthood provides counseling for pregnant teens.

don't give it to our daughters, they are the ones who will pay the price." In order to combat teen pregnancy, "parents, educators, and media need to speak honestly to teens about both the pleasures and pitfalls of sex," teen rights activist Rachel Kramer Bussel says. Bussel and others believe that when properly educated, many teens will choose wisely.

The controversy over who should be responsible for teenage sexuality and pregnancy is just one of the issues central to discussions about teen pregnancy. The viewpoints offered in *Introducing Issues with Opposing Viewpoints: Teen Pregnancy* will help to illuminate this and other aspects of this important and ongoing debate.

Chapter 1

Is Teen Pregnancy a Serious Problem?

Pregnancy at a young age can be challenging and overwhelming.

Viewpoint

1

Teen Pregnancy Is a Serious Problem

Hillary Rodham Clinton

"The U.S. has the highest teen pregnancy rate of any industrialized country."

Hillary Rodham Clinton is a U.S. senator from New York and the wife of former president Bill Clinton. The following viewpoint is an excerpt from a speech she gave to health care professionals in 2005. Clinton argues that pregnancy among youth is a serious problem in America. Teen pregnancy must be reduced immediately, Clinton says, by supporting national organizations that provide sex education and contraception to young women. Teens should also be encouraged to abstain from sex, but Clinton warns that because in reality many will still have sex, other prevention alternatives should be pursued.

GUIDED READING QUESTIONS:
1. What is the name of the organization Clinton helped her husband launch during the 1990s?
2. What percentage of teenage girls will become pregnant before their twentieth birthday, according to Clinton?
3. For what primary reason do teenage girls abstain from sex, according to the speech?

Hillary Rodham Clinton, "Remarks by Senator Hillary Rodham Clinton to the NYS Family Planning Providers," January 24, 2005. www.clinton.senate.gov.

We should all be able to agree that we want every child born in this country and around the world to be wanted, cherished, and loved. The best way to get there is do more to educate the public about reproductive health, about how to prevent unsafe and unwanted pregnancies. . . .

Supporting Teen Pregnancy Prevention

As many of you know, I have worked on these issues throughout my career and I continue to work on them in the Senate. One of the most important initiatives I worked on as First Lady and am proud

Senator Hillary Clinton believes sex education can help reduce teen pregnancy rates.

to continue to champion in the Senate is the prevention of teen pregnancy. I worked alongside my husband who launched the National Campaign to Prevent Teen Pregnancy in the mid-1990s. This organization, which has proven to be a tremendous success, was really was born out of my husband's 1995 State of the Union address, which declared teenage pregnancy to be one of the most critical problems facing our country. . . . .

I'm very proud of the work of the National Campaign. . . . and I will continue working with them to keep the number of unwanted pregnancies among our teenagers falling until we get to zero. But we have a long road ahead.

Fighting Teen Pregnancy

Today, even with the recent decline, 34% of teenage girls become pregnant at least once before their 20th birthday, and the U.S. has the highest teen pregnancy rate of any industrialized country. Children born to teen moms begin life with the odds against them. They are more likely to be of low-birth weight, 50 percent more likely to repeat

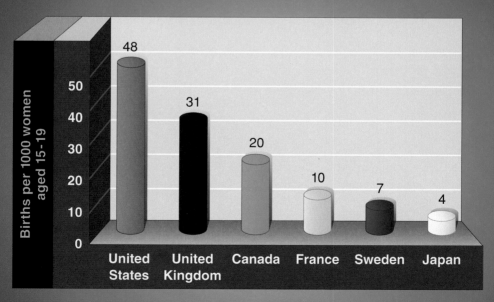

Teen Birth Rates in Selected Countries

Source: Population Resource Center, updated 2004.

a grade, and significantly more likely to be victims of abuse and neglect. And girls who give birth as teenagers face a long, uphill battle to economic self-sufficiency and pride. Clearly we do have our work cut out for us.

Research shows that the primary reason that teenage girls abstain is because of their religious and moral values. We should embrace this—and support programs that reinforce the idea that abstinence at a young age is not just the smart thing to do, it is the right thing to do. But we should also recognize what works and what doesn't work, and to be fair, the jury is still out on the effectiveness of abstinence-only programs. I don't think this debate should be about ideology, it should be about facts and evidence—we have to deal with the choices young people make not just the choice we wish they would make. We should use all the resources at our disposal to ensure that teens are getting the information they need to make the right decision.

Parental Roles

We should also do more to educate and involve parents about the critical role they can play in encouraging their children to abstain from sexual activity. Teenagers who have strong emotional attachments to their parents are much less likely to become sexually active at an early age.

But we have to do more than just send the right messages and values to our children. Preventing unwanted pregnancy demands that we do better as adults to create the structure in which children live and the services they need to make the right decisions.

The Tools for Preventing Teen Pregnancies

A big part of that means increasing access to family planning services. . . .

It's also important that private insurance companies do their part to help reduce unwanted pregnancies. That is why I am a proud

Signe Wilkinson. Reproduced by permission.

co-sponsor of the Equity in Prescription Insurance and Contraceptive Coverage—the so-called EPICC. The legislation would require private health plans to cover FDA-approved prescription contraceptives and related medical services to the same extent that they cover prescription drugs and other outpatient medical services. . . .

Contraception is basic health care for women, and the burden for its expense cannot fall fully on all women, many who after all live below that poverty rate, and in many instances above it, but not by very much and have a hard time affording such prescriptions. . . . The U.S. has one of the highest rates of unintended pregnancy in the industrialized world. Each year, nearly half of the six million pregnancies in this country are unintended, and more than half of all unintended pregnancies end in abortion.

The use of contraception is a big factor in determining whether or not women become pregnant. In fact, this is a statistic that I had not known before we started doing the research that I wanted to include in this speech, 7% of American women who do not use contraception account for 53% of all unintended pregnancies. So by preventing unintended pregnancy, contraception reduces the need for abortion. Improving insurance coverage of contraception will make contraception more affordable and reduce this rate of abortion. . . .

Helping Women and Girls Make Good Decisions

I think it's important that family planning advocates reach out to those who may not agree with us on everything to try to find common ground in those areas where, hopefully, emergency contraception, more funding for prenatal care and others can be a point of common ground.

As an advocate for children and families throughout my life, as a lawyer who occasionally represented victims of sexual assault and rape, as a mother, as a wife, as a woman, I know the difference that good information, good education, and good health care can make in empowering women and girls to make good decisions for themselves.

EVALUATING THE AUTHOR'S ARGUMENTS:

In this viewpoint, author Hillary Rodham Clinton addresses people who provide services to pregnant women and teenagers. In the following viewpoint, author David Brooks addresses the readers of the *International Herald Tribune*. Review the two articles' main arguments. Now consider whom each author is addressing. Does considering the authors' audiences change your opinion of their arguments? How?

Teen Pregnancy Is No Longer as Serious a Problem

"There's been a distinct rise in the number of teenagers who think casual sex is wrong."

David Brooks

David Brooks is a conservative opinion columnist for the *New York Times* as well as a contributor to magazines such as the *Weekly Standard, Newsweek,* and the *Atlantic Monthly.* In the following viewpoint, he argues that teen pregnancy is on the decline. Brooks contends that, despite living in a sex-infused popular culture, teens have learned from the mistakes of their elders and often refrain from self-destructive behavior, including casual sex. American youths are making healthy decisions and should be applauded, he concludes.

GUIDED READING QUESTIONS:
1. By how much have teen pregnancy rates declined over the past fifteen years, according to the author?
2. What is the definition of *heterodoxical*?
3. What is one specific reason given by the author for the decline in teen pregnancy?

You see the febrile [feverish] young teens in their skintight spaghetti strap tank tops. You hear the rapper 50 Cent's ode to oral sex, "Candy Shop," throbbing form their iPods. You open the university newspapers and see the bawdy sex columns.

You could get the impression that America's young people are leading lives of . . . hedonism. You could give credence to all those parental scare stories about oral sex parties at bar mitzvahs and junior high school dances. You could worry about hookups, friends with benefits, and the rampant spread of casual, transactional sexuality.

But it turns out you'd be wrong.

Some argue that sexual songs by 50 Cent (pictured) and other artists do not lead teens to have sex.

Teen Pregnancy Has Declined

The fact is, sex is more explicit everywhere in America on television shows like "Desperate Housewives," on booty-quaking music videos, on the Internet except in real life. As the entertainment media have become more sex-saturated, American teenagers have become more sexually abstemious [moderate].

Teenage pregnancy rates have declined by about a third over the past 15 years. Teenage birth and abortion rates have dropped just as much.

Young people are waiting longer to have sex. The percentage of 15-year-olds who have had sex has dropped significantly. Among 13-year-olds, the percentage has dropped even more.

Some studies indicate that teens today have fewer partners and are waiting longer to have sex.

They are also having fewer partners. The number of high school-ers who even report having four or more sexual partners during their lives has declined by about a quarter. Half of all high school boys now say they are virgins, up from 39 percent in 1990.

A More Moral Culture

Reports of an epidemic of teenage oral sex are also greatly exaggerated. There's little evidence to suggest it is really happening. Meanwhile, teenagers' own attitudes about sex are turning more conservative.

There's been a distinct rise in the number of teenagers who think casual sex is wrong. There's been an increase in the share of kids who think teenagers should wait until adulthood before getting skin to skin.

FAST FACT

Nine out of ten thirteen- to fourteen-year-olds said they disapproved of kids their age having sex, according to a 2005 poll by Princeton Survey Research Associates.

When you actually look at the intimate life of America's youth, you find this heterodoxical pattern: People can seem raunchy on the surface but are wholesome within. There are Ivy League sex columnists who don't want anybody to think they are loose. There are foul-mouthed readers of men's magazines like *Maxim* terrified they will someday divorce, like their parents. The rapper Eminem hardly seems like a paragon of traditional morality, but what he's really angry about is that he comes from a broken home, and what he longs for is enough suburban bliss to raise his daughter.

In other words, American pop culture may look trashy, but America's social fabric is in the middle of an amazing moment of improvement and repair.

Ending Old Fights

The first lesson in all this is we shouldn't overestimate the importance of the media. People like 50 Cent may produce hit after pornographic hit, but that doesn't mean his fans want to lead the lives he raps about. It's make-believe.

Open family discussions can encourage teens to make smart decisions regarding their health and sexuality.

What matters is reality. The reality is that a generation of kids have seen the ravages of divorce, are more likely to respect and listen to their parents and their ministers, are worried about sexually transmitted diseases and don't want to mess up their careers.

Second, it's becoming clear that we are seeing the denouement of one of the longest and increasingly boring plays on Broadway, the culture war.

Since the 1830s, America has witnessed the same struggle. One camp poses as the party of responsibility, lamenting the decadence of culture and the loss of traditional morality. The other side poses as the army of liberation, lamenting Puritanism, repression and the menace of the religious right.

No doubt some people will continue these stale . . . battles on into their graves: the '50s against the '60s, the same trumped-up outrage, the same self-congratulatory righteousness, the same fund-raising-friendly arguments again and again.

Youth Making Good Choices

But today's young people appear not to have taken a side in this war; they've just left it behind. For them, the personal is not political. Sex isn't a battleground in a clash of moralities.

They seem happy with the frankness of the left and the wholesomeness of the right. You may not like the growing influence of religion in public life, but the lives of young people have improved. You may not like the growing acceptance of homosexuality, but as it has happened heterosexual families have grown healthier.

Just lie back and enjoy the optimism.

EVALUATING THE AUTHOR'S ARGUMENTS:

In this viewpoint, author David Brooks states that we should "lie back and enjoy the optimism." Do you agree or disagree with this statement? Should society remain concerned about teen pregnancy or not? Support your answer with evidence from the viewpoint.

Improved Morality Has Reduced the Problem of Teen Pregnancy

Gene Edward Veith

"It has now become socially acceptable to be a virgin."

In the following viewpoint, Gene Edward Veith argues that the recently reported drop in teen pregnancies is due to an increased emphasis on morality among America's youth. More and more teens are taking virginity pledges, writes Veith, and those who do tend to delay sex longer and marry earlier—positive moral actions in Veith's view. The entertainment media and parents need to support the teens' recent decisions by curbing sexual messages, the author states.

Gene Edward Veith is the culture editor of the conservative religious magazine *World*. He has written a number of books on Christianity and modern life.

GUIDED READING QUESTIONS:
1. According to the Alan Guttmacher Institute report cited in the article, by how much did teenage pregnancy drop from 1990 to 2000?
2. Name one positive effect mentioned by the author of taking a virginity pledge.
3. How does the *New York Times* describe the new teen culture discussed in the article?

A reported drop in teen pregnancies is real and dramatic. And it's not because of abortion. More and more teenagers—and particularly boys—are changing their attitudes about premarital sex.

From 1990 to 2000, according to a study by the Alan Guttmacher Institute, teenage pregnancy dropped by 28 percent. The drop among black teenagers was even higher, 31.5 percent. (The current pregnancy rate averages 83.6 for every 1,000 teenagers.) The Guttmacher researchers estimate that 75 percent of the drop is due to increased use of contraceptives, but that 25 percent is due to more teenagers embracing abstinence.

Shift in Social Attitudes

Although most pregnancy-prevention programs focus on girls, *New York Times* reporter Nina Bernstein found that a great deal of the credit should go to boys, whose behavior shows the most startling changes. The conventional wisdom had been that boys will be boys and nothing can restrain their sexual appetites, but half of all male high-school students now say they are virgins, up from 39 percent in 1990. Sexual activity among teenage boys is down even in poor minority neighborhoods, where the problem of teen pregnancy has always been the worst.

It has now become socially acceptable to be a virgin. According to a Henry J. Kaiser Family Foundation study, 92 percent of all teens ages 15–17 believe that being a virgin in high school is a good thing. What motivates them to believe this, despite what the media and the entertainment industry are telling them? Researchers credit "a conservative religious movement" among teenagers. . . .

Effectiveness of Abstinence Pledges

Columbia University's Peter Bearman studied the sexual behavior of 12,000 adolescents over a period of six years. He found that the STD rate for those who made a virginity pledge was 2.8 percent, compared with 3.5 percent for those who did not, a statistical dead heat.

This sparked headlines across the world, to the effect that abstinence pledges are ineffective. But that is not what Mr. Bearman found. The pledges did delay sexual activity. The median age for first having

Some argue that teen pregnancy rates have dropped because more teenage boys are choosing not to have sex.

sex among girls who did not take the pledge was 16.7. For those who took the pledge, it was 19.9. Boys waited about the same time. (For black females, the ages were 16.3 for nonpledgers and 18.6 for those who pledged.) Pledgers also married at an earlier age.

"The delay effect is substantial and almost impossible to erase," wrote Mr. Bearman. "Taking a pledge delays intercourse for a long time. . . . The pledge effect is not a selection effect. It is real and it is substantial." This has a major impact on lower levels of teen pregnancy.

Pledges Reduce STDs

But what about sexually transmitted diseases? First of all, it is evident that those who keep their vows of chastity will not get them. The problem is not the pledge but a failure to keep the pledge. Of course, abstinence works, both to prevent pregnancy and to prevent diseases. If teenagers still have trouble staying abstinent, that is an argument for more abstinence education, not less.

But it is hard to resist temptation, and many pledgers eventually fall off the wagon. Mr. Pearson says that when that happens, many of the pledgers are less prepared to take measures against STDs, such as using condoms. (Never mind recent evidence that condoms do not, in fact, prevent STDs, except for AIDS.)

Still Need Improvement

Mr. Bearson's most disturbing statistics were that 99 percent of the teenagers who never pledged to remain a virgin have sex before they marry, and that 88 percent of those who did make the pledge eventually engage in premarital sex.

So despite the progress, we have a long way to go. It is not inevitable for adolescents to have sex. They can control their raging hormones, and they increasingly want to. They are working to create what *The New York Times* calls a "new teenage culture of restraint."

Society Needs to Help

The adults who make money from teenagers by selling them sexually charged music and other kinds of entertainment could help by showing some of that same restraint.

Despite the possible dangers of being sexually active, the decision not to have sex can be challenging for teens.

Christians know that the will is fallen, that simply choosing to be good will never be successful for long. Teenagers need the constant forgiveness of the gospel to bear fruit in sexual purity. The culture could also become more encouraging of early marriage, which is how most times and places have solved the problem.

At any rate, whatever the statistical flukes, teenagers are fighting their own culture war, and they deserve a great deal of credit.

EVALUATING THE AUTHOR'S ARGUMENTS:

In this viewpoint, author Gene Edward Veith states that teenagers have created "a new culture of restraint." In your opinion, do you think such a culture exists? Why or why not?

II A

Improved Social Programs Have Reduced the Problem of Teen Pregnancy

Tom Dennis

"[There is] more evidence that tough, deeply rooted social problems can be bent . . . by the winds of smart social and policy reforms."

In the following viewpoint, the author of an opinion editorial in a regional newspaper makes the argument that the recently reported drop in teen sex and pregnancies is due to improved social programs and government policy reforms. When teen pregnancy soared during the 1980s and 1990s, many new, strong programs were created, writes the author. The positive effects of those programs now are being demonstrated in the teen pregnancy decline.

Tom Dennis is an editor at the *Grand Forks Herald*, a North Dakota newspaper, from which this viewpoint was taken.

Take a minute today to ponder some very good news. "The teen birth rate reached a record low in 2002, dropping to the lowest level since the government started keeping records in the 1940s," the *Los Angeles Times* reported.

The drop is worth considering for all kinds of reasons. The first is that it was unexpected. Wouldn't you agree? Think about it: MTV videos remain as raunchy as ever, rock and hip-hop music blares lyrics that would be one long series of dashes if printed in this newspaper, and [radio DJ] Howard Stern offers up a nightly parade of exhibitionists so brazen that they want to strip not in a nightclub but on TV.

On top of that, the AIDS panic in America (and the sexual restraint it encouraged) has retreated as miraculous wonder drugs keep HIV-infected people heathy, seemingly indefinitely.

FAST FACT

Planned Parenthood, the largest reproductive health care program in the country, was founded in 1916 by contraception pioneer Margaret Sanger.

Face it, many said when confronted with these realities. The genie of human sexuality is out of the bottle—and there's no way society can put it back in.

Then, the teen birth rate goes and sets a new record low—the lowest since the bobby-sox days of the 1940s, mind you. Defying almost every signal from their surrounding media culture, it seems, "teens have been using contraceptives more often . . . and are having sex less often or abstaining entirely," the story reported.

Signe Wilkinson. Copyright © 2002 Signe Wilkinson. Reproduced by permission.

How to explain this newfound blend of modesty, morality and/or practicality among teens?

Improving Social Programs

A National Center for Health Statistics statistician hits on it: As the teen pregnancy rate jumped in the 1980s and 1990s, "people got really energized and started a whole lot of programs that got the teenagers' attention," Stephanie Ventura said.

So, there it is again: More evidence that tough, deeply rooted social problems can be bent (if not broken) by the winds of smart social and policy reforms.

Americans relearn this again and again, but the lesson is fresh and inspiring every time. Remember stagflation? The combination of high inflation and high unemployment made the late 1970s a miserable time and helped bring about President Jimmy Carter's famous speech about a "national malaise."

Then, the 1980s saw Ronald Reagan in the White House and Paul Volcker . . . at the Federal Reserve, and both inflation and unemployment dropped.

Of course, the 1980s had their own share of "intractable" problems: American cities spawned a seemingly permanent underclass, for example, and exploded in an orgy of crime. By 1988, the New York subways had become such a Stygian underworld that the gates could have featured the slogan, "Abandon all hope, ye who enter here."

But the 1990s brought fundamental welfare and law-enforcement reforms that made crime and the cycle of poverty recede.

An abundance of information and views on teen pregnancy is available on the Internet.

A Strong American Society

Now, it's [a] new millennium, and teen pregnancy's turn to reverse a trend and defy the odds.

This is a season of raw, gloves-off politics, with Republicans and Democrats slamming each other in speeches and attack ads. The Internet has opened up a whole new forum for dissent; at any time of day, Web loggers by the thousands are offering up their views of our world and its problems.

This cacaphony can seem unsettling and anarchic at times. But, by gosh, it works. It's a laboratory of democracy in which ideas get tested, and only the strongest survive.

In the long run, it enables American society to solve tough problems and advance.

And terrorists and dictatorships have nothing like it.

Amid the smorgasbord of temptations that the modern world offers, American teens behaved themselves in such a way as to make the teen birth rate drop. That's not only good news in its own right. It's an encouraging sign of how healthy American society remains.

EVALUATING THE AUTHOR'S ARGUMENTS:

The author of this viewpoint, Tom Dennis, and the author of the preceding viewpoint, Gene Edward Veith, both agree that the drop in teen pregnancy is a positive event. However, they disagree on the reasons for the drop. Consider each author's argument. Which do you find more compelling? Why?

Chapter 2

What Options Should Pregnant Teens Have?

The level of guidance parents should provide for their teens is hotly debated.

Viewpoint

1

Teens Should Have Access to Emergency Contraception

Liza Mundy

"For [teenage] girls, an after-the-fact form of contraception could be more crucial than for anybody."

In the following viewpoint, columnist Liza Mundy argues that emergency contraception (EC) should be available to teenagers without a prescription. Teens need access to emergency contraception the most, states Mundy, because they are the least likely to plan sex and the least likely to be prepared with birth control. The author concludes that emergency contraception has been proven to be a safe and effective drug and should be made available to prevent teen pregnancy.

Liza Mundy is a staff writer and columnist for the *Washington Post* and *Slate* online magazine. She writes on a variety of current events topics.

GUIDED READING QUESTIONS:

1. According to the author, how is the emergency contraception drug Plan B different from the drug RU-486?

Liza Mundy, "Dubious Conceptions," *http://www.slate.com*, June 1, 2004. Distributed by United Feature Syndicate, Inc. Reproduced by permission of the author.

2. What did Barr Laboratories researchers do to prove that women could safely take Plan B unsupervised?
3. According to Mundy, why is childbirth particularly undesirable for teenage girls?

In December [2003], an FDA advisory panel voted overwhelmingly in favor of making emergency contraception easily available, ruling that a drug called Plan B (levonorgestrel) should be sold in pharmacies without a prescription. It was a huge victory for reproductive rights groups, who went home exhilarated by the prospect that Plan B would soon materialize on drug store shelves, as easy to buy as Tylenol or Trojans or Slim-Fast.

In early May [2004], the acting director of the FDA's Center for Drug Evaluation and Research, Steven Galson, derailed that hope by nixing the application on the grounds that access to emergency contraception

Some advocates of emergency contraception would like to see it available for sale on drug store shelves.

might harm the very youngest teens. Plan B's proponents had failed, he said, to supply data about the drug's impact on "the younger age group from 11 to 14, where we know there's a substantial amount of sexual activity." It was a puzzling assertion, accompanying what many suspected was a politically motivated decision: There is plenty we don't know about young teens, but one of the things we do know is that they have very little sex at all. And what we know about the sex they are having only reinforces the case for making emergency contraception more available. As a reason for sabotaging efforts to take Plan B over-the-counter, Galson could hardly have reached for a more ironic one—and reach he certainly did.

Plan B Is Not an Abortion Pill

Emergency contraception, also known as the morning-after pill, is a highly effective form of hormonal birth control. Often wrongly confused with RU-486, EC does not induce abortion; instead, when taken

The Plan B pill prevents pregnancy from occurring after sex.

after unprotected sex or condom failure, it prevents pregnancy from occurring. For years women turned to Web sites to learn how to mix their own off-label EC, which is really just a cocktail of regular birth-control pills. Plan B was born when a woman named Sharon Camp formed a small company to distribute a dedicated EC product. In 1999 Plan B was approved for prescription use, but Camp had higher ambitions. If women could buy Plan B without having to ask a doctor first, she and others believed that it could cut America's abortion rate in half.

Plan B Can Be Taken Safely

It's a drug that works at its best when ready at hand. While EC can be taken up to 36 hours after intercourse, it's much more effective if taken right away, and its efficacy decreases with each passing hour. Most sex does not occur during doctors' working hours, so a quick prescription is hard to come by. Last year Camp's company was sold to Barr Laboratories, which agreed to spearhead an

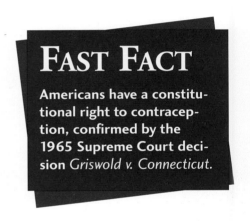

FAST FACT

Americans have a constitutional right to contraception, confirmed by the 1965 Supreme Court decision *Griswold v. Connecticut.*

over-the-counter campaign. As a prescription product, Plan B was already deemed safe and effective, so Barr's task was to show that women could safely take it unsupervised. Buttonholing women in shopping malls, researchers found women had no trouble reading the label. In family-planning clinics, a group of patients was given Plan B in advance, to gauge whether easy access would promote unsafe sex, but this did not turn out to be the case. . . .

Young Girls Should Not Get Pregnant

And let's consider those young, at-risk girls who are having sex despite efforts of right and left alike to dissuade them. Among this cohort, sex is least likely to be planned and least likely to be protected; stocking birth control "requires a level of planfulness that is not common at that age," as Kristen Moore, president of the research group Child Trends, puts it. For these girls, an after-the-fact form of contraception could be more crucial than for anybody.

It's also important to remember that the younger the girl, the more likely sex is to be coercive, usually forced on her by an older partner. According to the Alan Guttmacher Institute, seven out of 10 girls who have sex before the age of 13 do so involuntarily. These vulnerable teens are hardly in a position to make their partners wear a condom. Emergency contraception would give them a shot at staving off the consequences—consequences that hit young teenagers the hardest. It's often difficult for a young teen to get an abortion, thanks in part to parental notification and parental consent laws. Childbirth, too, is a terrible thing for this age group. Young teen mothers are least likely to

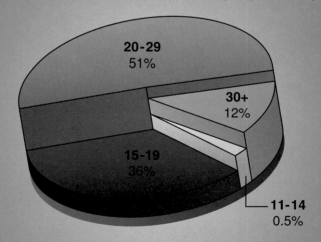

Emergency Contraception Users

A 2004 study conducted by Family Health International found that teenagers comprise 36 percent of women who request emergency contraception.

20-29
51%

30+
12%

15-19
36%

11-14
0.5%

Source: Family Health International study provided to FDA.

get prenatal care, most likely to deliver low birth-weight babies, and totally unprepared to be parents.

Information Is Difficult to Gather

Yet flimsy as it is, the young teen excuse is the one that Barr's company is going to have to deal with as it scrounges for the new information required to get the FDA to reconsider its "nonapprovable letter." One possibility Galson held out was for Barr to do a study assessing the effect of over-the-counter Plan B on the youngest girls. The trouble is that the federal government itself forbids researchers from talking about sex with this age group. CDC researchers, for example, must gather their data on young teens by asking older teens, retrospectively, about their first sexual encounter. Barr's researchers, when they first fanned out into those malls, were forbidden from interviewing unaccompanied teenagers, even older ones, which meant excluding what is arguably the most relevant portion of that age group. Even in family-planning clinics, Barr could not interview any lone teen under 14. In inviting further teen studies, Galson was asking the near-impossible.

It's no wonder that Carol Cox, a spokeswoman for Barr, says it will take too long to provide the data on young teens. Instead, the company will soon submit a plan to make Plan B over-the-counter for women 16 and older and available only by prescription to younger teenagers. This means, Cox acknowledges, that Plan B will almost certainly be stocked behind the register, not on the shelves. And that means any woman—of any age—will have to ask for it to get it, when *not* having to ask for it was the point to begin with.

EVALUATING THE AUTHOR'S ARGUMENTS:

The author of this viewpoint, Liza Mundy, argues that teens need unsupervised access to emergency contraception such as Plan B. The author of the following viewpoint, Elizabeth Bossom, states that teenagers should not have access to emergency contraception without a prescription. After reading both viewpoints, do you think teenagers should be allowed to take emergency contraception unsupervised? Why or why not?

Teens Should Not Have Access to Emergency Contraception

Elizabeth Bossom

"In cases where fertilization has already occurred, the morning-after pill could likely kill a developing embryo."

In the following viewpoint, author Elizabeth Bossom argues that allowing teenagers access to emergency contraception is both immoral and dangerous. In certain cases emergency contraception can be considered an abortifacient—a drug that causes an abortion—which the author believes to be inherently wrong. In addition, Bossom argues that women and girls may abuse the pills if not supervised by a doctor, thus increasing their chances of dangerous complications.

Elizabeth Bossom is an opinion columnist for Concerned Women for America, a conservative public advocacy group that focuses on family values. She writes frequently on current women's issues in the media.

GUIDED READING QUESTIONS:

1. According to the author, what protection does the morning-after pill offer against sexually transmitted diseases?

Elizabeth Bossom, "Contraception or Deception?," *www.cwfa.org*, March 8, 2006. Reproduced by permission.

2. What are the names of the two products approved for use as morning-after pills?
3. What is one side effect of taking the morning-after pill regularly, according to Dr. John Diggs?

W hile many American women have never heard of the morning-after pill, those who are familiar with it are often vocal and passionate—whether they are advocates or critics. Several female politicians, including Sen. Hillary Clinton (D-New York), want to use your tax money to promote this little-known but highly controversial pill. On the other hand, some nurses and pharmacists would rather lose their jobs than be forced to provide women and teenagers with the morning-after pill.

What is it about this tiny pill that causes such turmoil? The morning-after pill, also referred to as emergency contraception or postcoital contraception, is usually prescribed after sex with failed or no contraception. When taken within 72 hours of sexual intercourse, the morning-after pill is 75–85 percent effective in preventing conception or possibly ending an early pregnancy.

Just Another Form of Abortion?

According to the American College of Obstetricians and Gynecologists (ACOG), "Use of emergency contraception could prevent as many as 1.5 million of the approximately 3 million unintended pregnancies that occur each year in the United States." However, many concerned medical professionals argue that this controversial product does not necessarily prevent pregnancy. They believe that, at least in some cases, it kills a developing embryo. And that would make it an abortifacient, a way to kill an unborn child.

Two products approved by the Food and Drug Administration are dedicated for use as morning-after pills, namely Preven and Plan B. . . .

Marketing Misinformation to Teens

Aside from the morning-after pills' abortifacient potential, the strategy used to market it is of great concern. In the United States, teenagers are able to get a prescription for the morning-after pill without parental knowledge or consent at Planned Parenthood or other "family planning" clinics.

Is it morally justifiable to market the morning-after pill to minors?

The marketers of Plan B developed ads to be placed in college newspapers and hung on dorm room walls. One ad featured a shirtless male model and the following text:

> Of all the things you'd love to hear him whisper in your ear, "Oops—the rubber broke" isn't one of them. Condoms, like men, aren't perfect. Unfortunately a condom's imperfections aren't cute or lovable. . . . Find out how morning-after contraception, taken within 72 hours after intercourse, can be your back-up plan in preventing pregnancy. ACCIDENTS HAPPEN. That's why there's morning-after contraception.

A young woman stops to look at a variety of birth control advertisements, some of which can be confusing or misleading.

Abortion promoters realize that if they can attract a young woman, they may have a client for life. . . .

Promotions of the morning-after pill acknowledge the faults of condoms, the only tool "family planning" agencies tout for disease prevention. The morning-after pill provides no protection from any of the 25 (at least) known sexually transmitted diseases, including HIV, human papillomavirus, chlamydia, herpes, gonorrhea, genital warts, syphilis and hepatitis B.

Reviews of 16 recent print advertisements for "emergency contraceptives" show zero references to the lack of protection from sexually transmitted diseases.

Teenagers, the target audience of many "emergency contraception" advertisements, are notoriously worried about pregnancy but may have very little knowledge about diseases contracted by sexual activity. "Family planning" groups need to do more to convey the seriousness and prevalence of STDs. To prey upon or perpetuate that ignorance does America's children a grave disservice. . . .

A pharmacist takes a call to fill an emergency contraception prescription.

Dangerous Health Risks

Currently, ACOG urges doctors to prescribe the morning-after pill ahead of time, so that women have a "just-in-case" dose of the pills readily available in their medicine closets.

Abortion providers would like even fewer restrictions on the availability of "emergency contraception." In most states, the prescription, as with all birth control pills, must come from a doctor. In 2001, a group of organizations, including NARAL [the National Abortion and Reproductive Rights Action League] and the American Medical Association, requested that the FDA drop this safety requirement.

FAST FACT

One emergency contraceptive pill contains ten to fifteen times the level of estrogen found in a single day's dose of a birth control pill.

"The American Medical Association is now pushing to make emergency contraception an over-the-counter product, like Tylenol or Sudafed," wrote Janelle Brown in a feature for *Salon.com* magazine.

Not everyone is comfortable with the thought of women getting the pills without seeing a doctor. Dr. John Diggs, spokesman for the Consortium of State Physician Resource Councils, says:

> Other medical issues are ignored. If the cocktail is over-the-counter (available without a prescription), then there [is] no limit on how often the pills can be used. Consequently, some women will essentially be taking high-dose hormones regularly, which may increase the frequency of catastrophic side effects of these drugs—stroke, life-threatening blood clots. . . .

Tragedy in Britain

In Great Britain, the morning-after pill is available without a prescription. In fact, in an effort to lower the teen birthrate, Britain has gone so far as to use public funds to enable women under 20 to walk into local pharmacies and pick up free doses of the morning-after pill. Meanwhile, *The London Times* reported an epidemic of sexually

A mother and daughter discuss birth control options.

transmitted diseases among British teenagers, with skyrocketing diagnoses of the diseases among teens over a five-year period.

Throwing the morning-after pill at teenagers will never solve this problem. It is far less dangerous and more effective to share with teenagers the concept that sex is a wonderful experience for couples to share with each other when they have the security of matching wedding bands. How misguided that the British government should choose to fund a morally controversial program that fails to reduce adolescent sexual activity and sexually transmitted diseases. . . .

Emergency Contraception Is Immoral

Even though "reproductive rights" groups are hyping the morning-after pill, it still is not widely used by American women. Only 6 percent of American women in a 2003 Kaiser Family Foundation survey said that they had ever used "emergency contraceptive pills," up from 2 percent in 2000. But as marketers launch advertising campaigns that omit important information, more and more uninformed American women may make decisions they will regret when they learn the facts.

In cases where fertilization has already occurred, the morning-after pill could likely kill a developing embryo. When this is the case, serious ethical concerns arise. Sincere, upstanding citizens and health care providers who morally object to use of the morning-after pill should be free to abide by their convictions without threat of losing their livelihood.

Women have a right to know the controversy surrounding the morning-after pill so that they may make informed decisions. Concerned Women for America urges women to consider the facts and to make decisions that respect the lives of human beings, even in their earliest stages.

EVALUATING THE AUTHOR'S ARGUMENTS:

The author of the viewpoint you just read believes that emergency contraception should not be widely used. However, she also cites a statistic that states that 1.5 million accidental pregnancies could be prevented by using emergency contraception. Considering what you have read on the subject, do you think that emergency contraception should be widely available if it is capable of preventing so many accidental pregnancies? Why or why not?

Teens Should Need Parental Permission to Have an Abortion

"The right of parents to protect the health and welfare of their minor daughters needs to be protected."

Marcia Carroll

In the following viewpoint, Marcia Carroll, the mother of a pregnant teenager, argues that it should be illegal for minors to have an abortion without their parents' permission. Carroll's daughter initially chose to have her baby; however, without Carroll's approval, the family of her daughter's boyfriend took her to have an abortion in a state that did not require parental permission. The girl later regretted terminating the pregnancy. Carroll uses her daughter's story to argue that if parental consent laws had been in place in their neighboring state, her daughter could not have been forced to have an abortion there. She concludes that Congress should protect a parent's right to protect his or her child's health by requiring doctors to obtain parental consent before performing abortions on minors.

Marcia Carroll, "Marcia Carroll, "Testimony in Support of HR 748, the Child Interstate Notification Act"," *Subcommittee on the Constitution, U.S. House of Representatives*, March 3, 2005. Reproduced by permission.

GUIDED READING QUESTIONS:
1. What does the Pennsylvania Abortion Control Act require, as reported by the author?
2. What state does Carroll's daughter live in? To what state was she taken to have the abortion?
3. How has Carroll's daughter been affected by this experience, as reported by the author?

O n Christmas Eve 2004, my daughter informed me she was pregnant. I assured her I would seek out all resources and help that was available. As her parents, her father and I would stand beside her and support any decision she made. . . .

My daughter chose to have the baby and raise it. My family fully supported my daughter's decision to keep her baby and offered her our love and support.

A conversation about an unplanned pregnancy can be difficult and painful.

Subsequently, her boyfriend's family began to harass my daughter and my family. They started showing up at our house to express their desire for my daughter to have an abortion.

My Daughter Was Pressured and Threatened

When that did not work, his grandmother started calling my daughter without my knowledge. They would tell her that if she kept the baby, she couldn't see her boyfriend again. They threatened to move out of state.

I told his family that my daughter had our full support in her decision to keep the baby. She also had the best doctors, counselors, and professionals to help her through the pregnancy. We all had her best interests in mind.

The behavior of the boy's family began to concern me to the point where I called my local police department for advice. Additionally, I called the number for an abortion center to see how old you have to be to have an abortion in our state.

FAST FACT

In a Fox News poll, 78 percent of registered voters surveyed said they supported parental notification laws for teen abortions.

I felt safe when they told me my minor daughter had to be 16 years of age in the state of Pennsylvania to have an abortion without parental consent. I found out later that the Pennsylvania Abortion Control Act actually says that parental consent is needed for a minor under 18 years of age.

They Took My Daughter Against Her Will

It never occurred to me that I would need to check the laws of other states around me. I thought as a resident of the state of Pennsylvania that she was protected by Pennsylvania state laws. Boy, was I ever wrong.

On Feb. 16th, I sent my daughter to her bus stop with $2.00 of lunch money. I thought she was safe at school. She and her boyfriend even had a prenatal class scheduled after school.

However, what really happened was that her boyfriend and his family met with her down the road from her bus stop and called a

A doctor and a pregnant teen discuss the available options.

taxi. The adults put the children in the taxi to take them to the train station.

His stepfather met the children at the train station, where he had to purchase my daughter's ticket since she was only fourteen. They put the children on the train from Lancaster to Philadelphia. From there, they took two subways to New Jersey. That is where his family met the children and took them to the abortion clinic, where one of the adults had made the appointment.

"They Left Her Alone During the Abortion"

When my daughter started to cry and have second thoughts, they told her they would leave her in New Jersey. They planned, paid for, coerced, harassed, and threatened her into having the abortion. They left her alone during the abortion and went to eat lunch.

After the abortion, his stepfather and grandmother drove my daughter home from New Jersey and dropped her off down the road from our house.

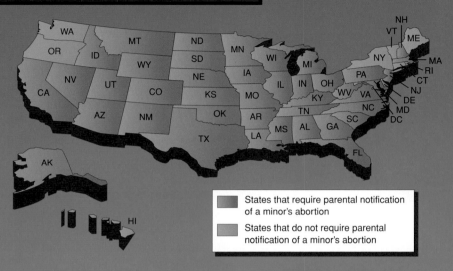

Parental Notification of Minors' Abortions

States that require parental notification of a minor's abortion

States that do not require parental notification of a minor's abortion

Source: The Alan Guttmacher Institute, www.guttmacher.org, March 2006.

My daughter told me that on the way home she started to cry, they got angry at her and told her there was nothing to cry about.

Anything could have happened to my daughter at the abortion facility or on the ride back home. These people did not know my daughter's medical history, yet they took her across state lines to have a medical procedure without my knowledge or consent. Our family will be responsible for the medical and psychological consequences for my daughter as a result of this procedure that was completed unbeknownst to me.

I was so devastated that this could have been done that I called the local police department to see what could be done. They were just as shocked and surprised as I was that there was nothing that could be done in this horrible situation.

Parental Consent Laws Protect Our Children

The state of Pennsylvania does have a parental consent law. Something has to be done to prevent this from happening to other families. This is just not acceptable to me and should not happen to families in this country. If your child goes to her school clinic for a headache, a registered nurse can't give her a Tylenol or aspirin without a parent's written permission.

As a consequence of my daughter being taken out of our state for an abortion without parental knowledge, she is suffering intense grief. My daughter cries herself to sleep at night and lives with this everyday.

I think about what I could or should have done to keep her safe. Everybody tells me I did everything I could have and should have done. It doesn't make me feel any better, knowing everything I did was not enough to protect my daughter.

The right of parents to protect the health and welfare of their minor daughters needs to be protected.

EVALUATING THE AUTHOR'S ARGUMENTS:

In this viewpoint, the author uses a personal story to make her argument that teens should need parental permission in order to have an abortion. Do you find this method to be persuasive? Why or why not? Compare this style of writing with other styles demonstrated in this book.

Teens Should Not Need Parental Permission to Have an Abortion

Richard Pan

"Mandatory notification laws . . . leave girls in need alone, frightened and in real danger."

In the following viewpoint, author Richard Pan, a pediatrician and vice chairman of the California Medical Association's Council on Legislation, argues that requiring girls to get permission before an abortion would undermine the trust between girls and their doctors. Many girls cannot talk to their parents, Pan points out, especially those in abusive homes. He warns that parental notification laws would restrict girls' access to safe abortions, perhaps leading them to try more dangerous methods of ending their pregnancies.

Editor's note: Proposition 73 failed during the November 2005 election; however, a petition has been circulated to reintroduce it in November 2006.

GUIDED READING QUESTIONS:
1. According to the author, how much have teen pregnancy rates dropped in California since 1995?
2. What do proponents of the initiative say an abused teen should do if she is pregnant? Why does the author believe this is unrealistic?
3. What is the name of one organization that opposes Proposition 73?

A s a pediatrician who cares for teens in my Sacramento [California] practice . . . I strongly encourage parents to be involved in their teenagers' lives. Studies have shown that parents are the primary influence in their sons' and daughters' lives.

Every day, parents and teens talk to me and other physicians about their concerns when it comes to the outside influences affecting teens— peer pressure, television, smoking and so on. Parents want their teens to be healthy, happy and successful, and to share their values. But no law is going to force a teen to talk to her parents. Proposition 73 [which proposed requiring teens to have parental permission for an abortion] will not build the trust essential among teens, their parents and their doctors to assure parents the safety and health of their child.

Not Always Possible to Talk to Parents

The best way to protect our daughters, of course, is to talk to them. It isn't easy to talk to your kids about sex. But parents are talking to their teens, and as a result teen pregnancy rates in California have dropped 40 percent [since 1995].

As a physician, I know teens who come from homes with good family relationships and who are too embarrassed to talk to their

> **FAST FACT**
>
> On September 16, 1998, seventeen-year-old Becky Bell of Missouri died of complications that resulted from an unsafe, illegal abortion, which she sought in an attempt to avoid telling her parents she was pregnant, as was required by state law.

parents about something as sensitive as sex and pregnancy. They don't want to disappoint their families.

And in troubled homes, some teens simply can't talk to their parents because they fear being physically harmed or expelled from their home if they disclosed an unplanned pregnancy. Still more tragic is the situation where the child may be abused by a family member, or a friend of the family or stepparent. This child often has nowhere to turn within the family and seeks the advice and treatment of a physician—and rightly so.

Teens Need Free Abortion Access

Physicians need to provide that help. Proposition 73, however, threatens physicians with being criminals for doing so, and actual-

Feelings of sadness and loneliness can occur when teens feel they cannot discuss serious issues with their parents.

Doctors can provide information, comfort, and help for pregnant teens.

ly puts those vulnerable teenagers—those who most need help—in harm's way.

The proponents [supporters] of this initiative will tell you that an abused teen can and should go to court. Both they and we all know that's unrealistic. A frightened, pregnant teen is unlikely to find a courthouse and go through a legal proceeding to do this. She doesn't need a judge; she needs a trusted counselor and a caring medical professional.

Teens' Safety at Stake

With nowhere to turn, the teen would likely seek no solution at all, resulting in an unwanted and surprise pregnancy, or a dangerous alternative, such as an abortion by a nonprofessional, drugs or suicide. . . .

That's why organizations that represent the medical community—the American Academy of Pediatrics, the California Nurses Association, the California Medical Association and the Academy of Family Physicians—all oppose Proposition 73.

Mandatory notification laws sound good by providing a false sense of control over a teen, but, in the real world, they leave girls in need alone, frightened and in real danger.

EVALUATING THE AUTHOR'S ARGUMENTS:

In the previous viewpoint, Marcia Carroll states that parental permission should be required for teens to have abortions. In this viewpoint, Richard Pan argues that teens should be able to have abortions without parental permission. After reading both viewpoints, which argument do you agree with? State your reasons.

Teen Mothers Can Give Their Babies Up For Adoption

Krissy Stautz

"'I was 100-percent comfortable with having these people raise my child.'"

Krissy Stautz is a seventeen-year-old student and writer from Oregon. In the following viewpoint, she makes the point that ending a pregnancy is not the only option available for pregnant teenagers. Adoption is also a viable choice that is right for some girls. Stautz tells the story of one pregnant teen who considered abortion but chose to give her baby up for adoption. The teen felt good about her choice, Stautz writes, because she was able to choose the adoptive parents herself and form a relationship with them, as well as maintain contact with her baby.

GUIDED READING QUESTIONS:
1. What is open adoption, as described by the viewpoint?
2. Why did Tamera feel she was not ready to be a parent?
3. What services do adoption agencies typically offer to birth mothers?

Krissy Stautz, "No Secrets: Open Adoption Shuts Out the Shame," *www.sexetc.org*, July 21, 2004. Reproduced by permission.

I t's a story baby Henry will surely hear over and over again. And when he's old enough to understand, the words "birth mother" and "open adoption" will be as normal to him as "mom" and "dad."

The story starts with a young woman named Tamera Alvarez, who lives in California. She was 18 when she discovered she was pregnant. She and the baby's father were best friends who dated for a few months.

Abortion Is Not Right for Everyone

Tamera knew she couldn't raise a child alone, but was unsure about what she wanted to do.

Many pregnant teens wrestle with the choice of putting their babies up for adoption.

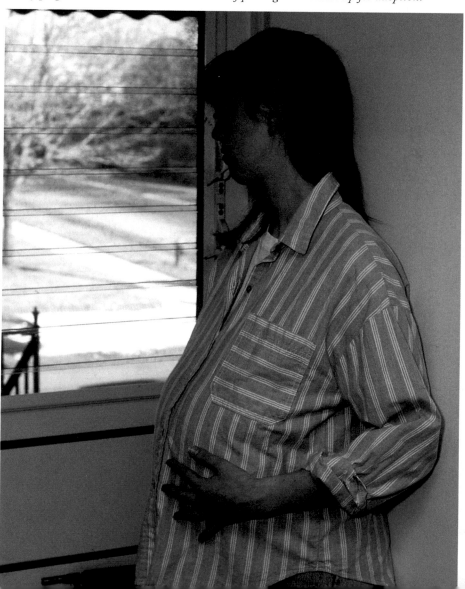

A distraught couple discusses the options for dealing with their unplanned pregnancy.

"I was ignorant when it came to open adoption," she says. "Originally, I considered abortion."

But the more she peeled apart her feelings, the more she realized abortion was the wrong choice for her. So, she researched her options.

Adoption Can Meet Everyone's Needs

In a town just a few miles from where Tamera lived, husband and wife Jan Newberry and Carroll Moore were writing a letter to a birth mother they had not yet met.

They were filling out papers at the Independent Adoption Center in Pleasant Hill, CA. As Tamera was going through morning sickness, struggling to finish high school, and filling out college applications, Jan and Carroll were praying for a child.

After weeks of soul searching, Tamera decided that keeping the baby would be unfair. She could never give the child the life it deserved. Tamera and her boyfriend, Eric, chose to create an adoption plan for their child.

"At first, I planned to just give the baby up and forget about it," says Tamera. "I thought that would be easier for me and the baby."

Then she discovered open adoption.

"Everything Just Seems Perfect"

Open adoption allows birth mothers to choose their child's adoptive parents. Typically, they meet the parents and work out an agreement to keep in touch. For some, that means yearly letters. For others, it means regular visits.

For Tamera, open adoption seemed like the best solution.

So, she began wading through more than 150 letters from possible adoptive parents.

Finally, Tamera narrowed it down to three potential parents and arranged meetings with them. When she met Carroll and Jan, something clicked.

"The thing I liked right away about them was how open they were about everything," Tamera says, comparing her relationship with Jan and Carroll to falling in love.

"It was like that feeling when everything just seems perfect and you feel like you've known them forever."

No Shame in Adopting

Jan said she and her husband wanted an open adoption from the beginning. She wanted her son to know where he came from. And she wanted to take the shame out of adoption.

"We didn't want any secrets," Jan says. "Henry will grow up knowing all this, and he'll accept it. We're giving up the drama that goes with adoption."

Jan and Carroll attended the required counseling sessions at the adoption center, went to birthing classes with Tamera, and were by her side when Henry was born.

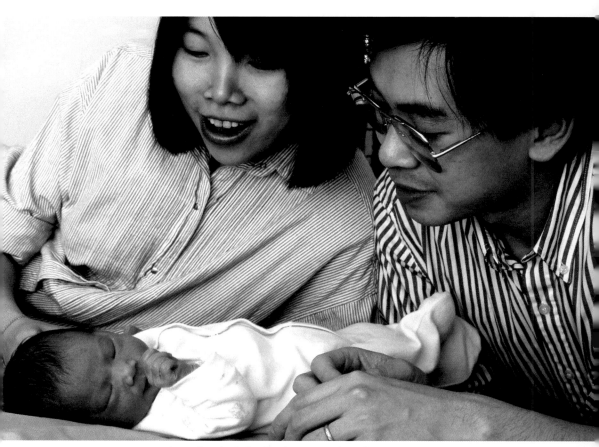

New parents joyously tend to the baby they have just adopted.

They became a family—not a conventional one—but one created out of love and a need for each other.

"Tamera is great," says Jan. "We really love her a lot."

"After just four or five months, I was 100-percent comfortable with having these people raise my child," adds Tamera, who now has a new boyfriend, is attending school, and living the life of a typical teenager. "They were ready to be parents. I wasn't.

"I won't lie and say it was easy for me," admits Tamera. "But knowing where he is right now and that, in 10 minutes, I can be there, means a lot to me.". . .

Making the Choice

Adoption agencies typically give birth mothers free services, including counseling, legal fees and, in some cases, hospital fees, says Grace

Allen, outreach coordinator for the Independent Adoption Center, one of the largest open adoption agencies in the U.S.

Birth parents decide what they want in an adoptive family. They get letters from families that seem like a good fit, no matter where they live. Birth parents also review forms that adoptive parents fill out.

Once a match is made, both parties decide together what kind of relationship they want after the birth. They have a counselor who helps them come to an agreement that makes both sides happy.

Even though both parties sign the agreement, it does not give birth parents any legal right to the child or to visitation, explains Allen, whose agency arranged Henry's adoption. But in the nearly 20 years that the agency has been doing open adoptions, most people work out agreements that last a lifetime.

"Usually, it's a win-win situation," says Allen.

EVALUATING THE AUTHOR'S ARGUMENTS:

In this viewpoint, a pregnant teenager, Tamera, states that keeping her baby would have been unfair, because she could not have provided it with the life it deserved. Do you agree or disagree with this statement? In your opinion, can teen mothers provide good homes for their babies? Why or why not?

Chapter 3

How Should Teen Pregnancy Be Prevented?

A group of high school students participates in a heated discussion during a sex education class.

Sex Education Should Be Taught in Schools

"Education is the strongest tool society has for helping teens deal with the physical and emotional repercussions of sex."

Kathryn Chinn

In 2005 Kathryn Chinn was a senior at Grand Junction High School in Grand Junction, Colorado. She wrote the following viewpoint as an opinion editorial for the *Denver Post*. Chinn argues that sex education should be taught in the classroom to kids of all ages. A large percentage of teenagers are sexually active already, she points out, and even young children are aware of sex from television and movies. Instead of ignoring the reality that sex is everywhere, Chinn writes, we should educate children and teenagers about how to protect themselves from diseases and pregnancy. The schools are the natural place for this discussion to happen, she concludes.

GUIDED READING QUESTIONS:

1. In 1995 what was the percentage of Colorado students who had had sex, according to the statistics in the article?

2. At what point in their school career should children begin learning about sex, according to the author?
3. What percentage of Americans believe sex education should not be taught in schools, as reported by Chinn?

I have not had sex. As a high school senior, that fact often makes me feel like an anomaly. Many teenagers are having sex; that cannot be denied. It's unfortunate, then, that they aren't given the tools to make better decisions about when to have sex and how to handle the consequences.

Teenage sex is society's pink elephant. While everyone knows it's there, no one wants to discuss it—but it is not going away.

Many Teens Are Sexually Active

According to a 2003 survey by National Public Radio, the Kaiser Family Foundation and Harvard University's John F. Kennedy School of Government, 30 percent of schools teaching sex education focus on abstinence only. The thought behind this seems to be that if students are unaware of sex, they will not have it.

Yet teens are still aware enough about sex that some high schools have day-care centers. Teens are aware enough that "one in four sexually active teens contracts an STD every year," the Kaiser Foundation reported this year.

In Colorado, the percentage of students (excluding Denver) in 1995 who had had sex was approximately 46.6 percent, according to the Centers for Disease Control.

The Kaiser Foundation, meanwhile, in 2003 reported that 47 percent of ninth- to 12-graders nationwide had already had sex.

That's a lot of teens taking risks, many of whom don't have the information necessary to protect themselves.

While there is not a one-size-fits-all solution, education is the strongest tool society has for helping teens deal with the physical and emotional repercussions of sex. This may mean starting sex education in elementary school. (Another Kaiser Foundation study in 2002 found that 6 percent of girls and 8 percent of boys had initiated sexual intercourse before the age of 14.)

The Majority of Parents Favor Sex Education

Parents of High School Students

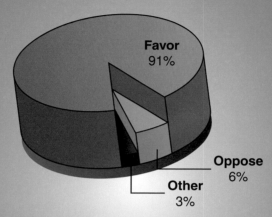

Favor
91%

Oppose
6%

Other
3%

Parents of Junior High School Students

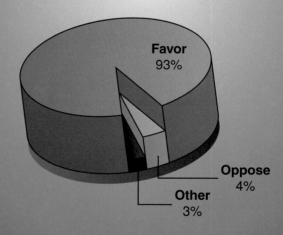

Favor
93%

Oppose
4%

Other
3%

Source: Siecus Fact Sheet: Public Support for Comprehensive Sexuality Education, Fall 2004.

Mixed Messages Are Confusing

Part of the problem is the mixed message that students receive starting in early childhood. Sex is everywhere, and children are exposed to it daily. Sex is at the newsstands, on TV and on the sides of buses.

At school, students are taught about abstinence. At night, they watch [the popular television series] "Sex and the City."

Parents and educators have to be aware of this. Sex in the media is not going to go away.

The solution to this mixed message must therefore start at home, where parents can explain the consequences and joys of relationships starting at a young age. As kids grow, so should the details and frequency of the discussions.

Classrooms Should Have Sex Education

However, sex education should also take place in the classroom, as part of a balanced curriculum, and must begin before hormones start

Television and other media bombard teens with messages about and images of sex.

to impede judgment. It then should continue into high school, giving students more information as they age, to help them to deal with new pressures and hormones.

Sex education needs to include not just the physical aspects—contraception, sexually transmitted diseases and pregnancy—but also the emotional aspects.

Knowing about the dangers of sex will probably not help every teenager just say "no." The hormonal and social pressures of high school are not generally conducive to that. Dating in high school and even middle school is huge.

However, knowing how to avoid STDs and pregnancy would go a long way toward keeping students healthy and reducing welfare claims of unwed teenage mothers. At St. Mary's Hospital in Grand Junction,

A teacher instructs her students during class. Debate rages whether sex education should be taught in schools.

more than 50 percent of births in 2004 were to mothers on Medicaid [the government program providing health coverage for low-income people].

We Must Talk About Sex

Only 7 percent of Americans believe that sex education should not be taught in school, according to the NPR-Kaiser-Harvard poll. Isn't it odd that students are endlessly warned of the dangers of drugs, but not the dangers of sex?

Sex education is not about politics; it is about common sense. Even if parents do not want their child learning about sex, what about other students who have not had the same moral upbringing and parental support to make good decisions? If a child does make a bad decision, should they not at least be informed about the consequences?

It is time for the elephant to become visible. Sex needs to be discussed frankly and openly so that children no longer get mixed messages and can make smart decisions with their bodies and their futures.

EVALUATING THE AUTHOR'S ARGUMENTS:

In this viewpoint, author Kathryn Chinn argues that schools are the natural place for kids to learn about sex. In the next viewpoint, author Kathleen Parker argues that parents should teach their kids about sex at home, and sex education should be kept out of schools. If you were going to write an essay on this topic, which position would you take? Support your answer with evidence from the viewpoints.

Sex Education Should Not Be Taught in Schools

Kathleen Parker

"When was it decided that children need to be fluent in sex? And why is it the government's job to teach it?"

Kathleen Parker is a syndicated columnist who frequently writes on family values, morality, and faith as well as politics and current events. In the following viewpoint, Parker argues that sex education should not be taught in schools. Government officials and educators who create sex education programs are assuming that children need to learn about sex. However, most children do not want or need to be educated about sex by their schools, maintains Parker, who worries that sex education classes force children to learn what they may not want to know. Sex is for parents to teach, not schools, she concludes.

GUIDED READING QUESTIONS:
1. What does the author think of a Yale and Columbia study about kids who pledge abstinence?
2. What is the author's problem with people who criticize abstinence programs as inadequate?
3. What assumption does Parker say underscores school sex education programs?

Kathleen Parker, "Making Sex Safe—and Boring," *www.townhall.com*, April 27, 2005. Reproduced by permission.

I n the history of unseemly trends, surely the current battle among adults over the intricacies of teen sex ranks near the top. Just reading the words "teen sex" sends me rocketing through wormholes of ennui [boredom].

I mean, really. Can't they just go outside and play? Not just the kids, but the grown-ups who refuse to leave them alone.

Perhaps this is just the wife in me talking, but surely no one thinks about sex as constantly as sex educators assume kids do. (If you disagree, please resist the urge to share.)

Adults Force the Issue of Sex on Kids

When it comes to the riveting issue of how we should teach kids to practice sex—safely, or not at all, or some combo thereof—it seems

High school students enjoy an engaging discussion. Some argue that parents, not schools, should provide sex education.

There is debate about how much information teens want regarding sex.

it's the adults who are consumed with sex, projecting their own obsession onto children, who have been denied the right *not* to know.

What was for other generations a mysterious and wondrous thing is now the equivalent of learning to change a tire in driver's ed. Only bureaucrats—and the world's increasingly wealthy condom vendors—could manage to make sex boring.

Badmouthing Abstinence

The latest addition to our nation's growing cognitive dissonance is a new study from Yale and Columbia universities that produced this nugget: Kids who pledge abstinence are more likely to have unsafe sex (when they finally give into the relentless societal pressure to canoodle).

Researchers report following 12,000 students in grades 7 through 12 for six years. They found that when those who had promised sexual abstinence did fall from grace, they were more likely not to use condoms than other kids. Ta-dum. Get it? If you want your kids to practice safe sex, better keep them away from those wacky abstinence programs.

Perhaps giving up abstinence for a roll in the hay is like abdicating Atkins [a popular diet that discourages eating carbohydrates] and scarfing several supersized orders of fries. Whatever the other confounding factors, the message seems clear: abstinence bad, condoms good. The subtext, of course, is that America's children can't control themselves, they must have sex, and therefore, they have to learn the nitty-gritty of the down 'n' dirty. Whether they want to or not.

We Should Not Teach Kids How to Have Sex

One does not have to be a hung-up, sexually repressed prude to feel nauseated by the triumph of Technos over Eros. Is not having sex ever an option for some who may prefer—oh, I dunno—an actual human relationship that leads to long-term commitment, perhaps marriage, wherein sex is an expression of spiritual intimacy rather than a mechanical engineering feat involving anatomical widgetry?

The Yale-Columbia study, published in the April [2005] issue of the Journal of Adolescent Health, has been released as Congress is reauthorizing abstinence-until-marriage block grants to states under welfare reform. Abstinence educators swear by their programs,

FAST FACT

Sex education programs in public schools began in the 1900s. The first formal protests against sex education began in the 1960s and were organized mainly by religious groups.

Mike Keefe. Reproduced by permission of Cagle Cartoons, Inc.

which teach the emotional, psychological and spiritual merits of post-poning sex. You know, like parents used to do. . . .

Those who find abstinence education woefully inadequate given assumptions that kids can't get through a day without sexual release prefer the comprehensive sex-ed curricula, which focus on contraception and protection against disease. Though abstinence is mentioned as an option, emphasis is on how-to, not how-not-to. . . .

Parents Should Teach Sex Ed, Not Schools

Recognizing that there's nothing new under the sun—and that sex is both pleasurable and a necessary human drive—could we neverthe-less stop panting long enough to ask whether any of this is sane? Since when was it decided that children need to be fluent in sex? And why is it government's job to teach it?

There are a hundred different arguments with the latest-breaking stats to match both for and against sex ed in school, but undergirding all the studies, curricula and rhetoric is another assumption that deserves closer scrutiny.

That is, that parents can't do a proper job of teaching their children values, morals and what we used to call the Birds 'n' the Bees, and that government bureaucrats are the last word on human intimacy.

Our children should fire us for dereliction of duty.

EVALUATING THE AUTHOR'S ARGUMENTS:

The author of this viewpoint, Kathleen Parker, believes that the government does not have the right to educate children about sex. Instead, she believes that is the right of parents. Do you agree or disagree with this argument? What role do you think the government should have in the lives of Americans?

Abstinence-Only Education Reduces Teen Pregnancy

Daniel Allott

"Teens' participation in sex education classes is associated with a higher risk of pregnancy and childbirth."

In the following viewpoint, author Daniel Allott argues that abstinence-only education is the best way to reduce teen pregnancy. Citing numerous reports and studies, he argues that sex education does not reduce teen sex rates because it sends the message that it is acceptable for kids to be having sex. He also believes sex education allows young people to falsely believe that as long as they use contraceptives correctly, they will not get pregnant or contract sexually transmitted disease (STD). Allott claims that abstinence-only education, on the other hand, firmly encourages kids to abstain from sex. Their abstinence protects them against teen pregnancy and STDs while also boosting their self-esteem. For these reasons, the author concludes that abstinence-only programs should be pursued in schools.

Daniel Allott is a policy analyst with American Values, the organization that published this viewpoint.

Daniel Allott, "Education Responsibility: Is Abstinence Education Best for Our Children?," *www.american values.org*, September 1, 2004. Reproduced by permission of the author.

GUIDED READING QUESTIONS:
1. According to the author, what effect does sexual activity have on depression and suicide rates?
2. What percentage of teenagers believe that teens should be taught abstinence, according to a poll reported in the viewpoint?
3. What did a Georgia study find about the effect of abstinence education on students, according to Allott?

D ebates concerning sex education have concentrated on two distinct approaches: "safe sex" courses allegedly teach at least some abstinence for teens but in fact primarily focus on teaching teens to use contraceptives, especially condoms, when having sex. A second approach, called abstinence education, promotes and encourages teens to delay sexual activity, usually until marriage. . . .

America's Teen Sex Problem

American adolescents still have pregnancy, birth and abortion rates twice as high as those in Canada and Great Britain, and three times as high as France and Sweden. Each year one million teenage women, ten percent of all women aged 15-19, become pregnant. Specifically:

- The likelihood of teenagers having intercourse increases steadily with age, however, about 80 percent of young people have intercourse as teenagers.
- The younger women are when they first have intercourse, the more likely they are to have had unwanted or involuntary first sex . . . 70 percent of those who had sex before age 13, for example.
- More than half (56 percent) of the 905,000 teenage pregnancies in 1996 ended in births (two-thirds of which were unplanned).

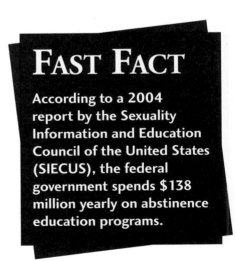

FAST FACT

According to a 2004 report by the Sexuality Information and Education Council of the United States (SIECUS), the federal government spends $138 million yearly on abstinence education programs.

In addition. . .

- Every year three million teens—about one in four sexually experienced teens—acquire an STD.

Sex Education's Failure

Sex education has been no panacea. Sex and contraceptive education is now available in over 90 percent of high schools and most teens are fully informed about how pregnancies occur. One problem is that no matter how well used, no contraceptive is perfect. In fact, with perfect use, the condom—the most commonly used contraceptive among teenagers—has a failure rate of three percent. Typical use failure rates are 15 percent for condoms, 30 percent for spermacides, and eight percent for the contraceptive pill.

Studies that examine the effects of teenage reports on sex education in schools are quite dubious. Some studies show that sex education is linked to decreased sexual activity, while others conclude that teens' participation in sex education classes is associated with a higher risk of pregnancy and childbirth. In addition, providing contraceptives to students via school-based health clinics is not always associated with earlier or increased sexual activity in teens but this practice has not been found to reduce pregnancy or birthrates for adolescents either. Surveys indicate that knowledge about contraceptives may give youth a false sense of security, not only from pregnancy but STDs.

In addition, contraceptives fail to take into account the possible emotional effects of teenage sexual activity. Teens who engage in pre-marital sex are likely to experience fear about pregnancy and STD's, guilt, regret, lowered self-respect, fear of commitment, and depression. Pre-marital sex can also cause teens to marry less favorably. A study of college freshman found that non-virgins with multiple sex partners were more likely to view marriage as difficult and involving a loss of personal freedom and happiness. Virgins were more likely to view marriage as enjoyable. Also, a 2003 Heritage Foundation study found that sexually active teenagers are more likely to be depressed and to attempt suicide, all else held equal. In fact, girls who were sexually active were three times as likely to attempt suicide (14 percent) than girls who were not sexually active in this study.

Some are concerned that teens who have premarital sex are less likely to want committed relationships later.

Abstinence: Preferred by Parents and Teens

Abstinence programs strongly encourage abstaining from sexual activity during the teen years, and preferably until marriage. They teach that casual sex at an early age not only poses serious threats of pregnancy and infection by STDs, but also can undermine an individual's capacity to build loving, intimate relationships as an adult, and interfere with their life goals, education, and career building. These programs encourage teen abstinence as a preparation and pathway to healthy adult marriage. . . .

There is little doubt that public opinion has progressed such that more parents and teens prefer abstinence education to traditional sex education. "Kids are saturated with information about contraception

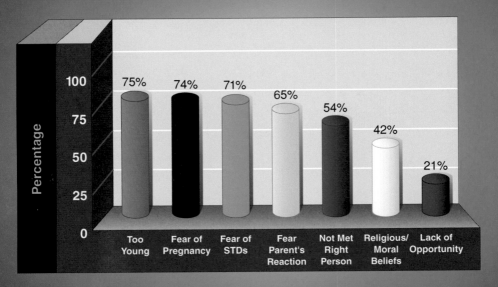

Reasons 13- to 16-Year-Olds Abstain from Sex

Percentage

75%	74%	71%	65%	54%	42%	21%
Too Young	Fear of Pregnancy	Fear of STDs	Fear Parent's Reaction	Not Met Right Person	Religious/ Moral Beliefs	Lack of Opportunity

Source: NBC News/*People* magazine poll conducted by Princeton Survey Research Associates, International, January 2005.

and messages about encouraging casual, permissive sex," said Robert Rector, who helped write the Bush administration's abstinence education program. In fact, teens want to be taught abstinence. A 2000 poll found that 93 percent of teenagers believe that teens should be given a strong message from society to abstain from sex until at least after high school. Parents, too, want their children to be taught that sex should be linked to marriage. Data drawn from a Zogby International poll of parents in December 2003 found that very few parents support basic themes of comprehensive sex-ed courses. In fact, 80 percent of parents want young people taught that sex should at least be delayed until after high school. And only seven percent want teens to be taught that sexual activity in high school is okay. Also, only eight percent of parents believed that teaching about contraceptives is more important than teaching about abstinence.

Abstinence Education Is Effective

According to the Physicians Resource Council, the drop in teen birth rates during the 1990's was due primarily to increased sexual abstinence. From 1988 to 1995, sexual activity among unwed boys aged 15 to 19 dropped from 60 to 55 percent. There are over 1000 abstinence until marriage programs in the United States. Most started by non-profit or faith-based organizations, these programs teach young people the skills needed to practice abstinence, including self-esteem building, self-control, decision-making, goal setting, character education and communication skills, and the reality of parenthood.

Despite opponents' assertions, abstinence programs have been proven to work. Choosing the Best, an abstinence program based in Georgia and started in 1993, developed a curriculum and materials that are used in over two thousand school districts in 48 states. The results have been quite notable. For example, Choosing the Best's materials were used in all 8th grade classes for a period of four years in certain school districts in Georgia. A study by the Georgia State Board of Education examined the effectiveness of this curriculum and found a 38 percent reduction in sexual activity among middle

Studies indicate that teens who participate in sports or other activities are less likely to be sexually active.

school students, while districts that didn't use abstinence-based education experienced an average of a six percent reduction during the same years.

Abstinence Leads to Healthy, Responsible Lives

In the end, sex education programs that teach teenagers about their bodies, but not how to deal with their feelings for one another and the values that should guide their relationships, fail. At the same time, "just say no" campaigns will not do much better if they fail to engage young people in constructive activities and offer alternatives to the pro-sex messages they are receiving from virtually every other influence in their lives. Experimental studies indicate that adolescents involved in community volunteer service programs and programs that focus on youth development, including involvement in such activities as educational mentoring, employment, sports, or the performing arts, have a strong impact on adolescent sexual activity. For the past two decades, contraceptives have been widely available to teens, and while pregnancy rates have declined, they are still much too high, and STDs are a problem that is beyond the scope of any contraceptive method. Abstinence until marriage education is the only way to ensure our children can lead healthy, responsible lives.

EVALUATING THE AUTHOR'S ARGUMENTS:

In this viewpoint, Daniel Allott argues that sex education programs give teenagers the message that having sex is acceptable; therefore, they cannot be effective against reducing rates of teenage sex. Do you agree with him? Do you think that programs that teach about contraception wrongly encourage kids to have sex, or do they provide them with useful information in the event that they have sex? Explain your answer.

Abstinence-Only Education Does Not Reduce Teen Pregnancy

"There is no credible evidence that abstinence-unless-married education delays sex or reduces teen pregnancy."

The National Family Planning and Reproductive Health Association

The following viewpoint is published by The National Family Planning and Reproductive Health Association, a nonprofit organization that supports comprehensive, culturally sensitive family planning and reproductive health care services. In the viewpoint, the association argues that abstinence-only education programs are not effective against reducing teen pregnancy rates. It claims that teaching kids solely about abstinence fails to prepare them for the realities of sexual intercourse. Although such programs may delay some teens from having sex for a little while, when they do have sex, they are unprepared to properly use contraception and thus wind up either pregnant or with

"Oppose Dangerous, Unproven Abstinence-Unless-Married Education Programs," *www.nfprha.org*, June 30, 2004. Reproduced by permission.

sexually transmitted diseases. The association laments the use of federal money to support abstinence programs that it believes do not properly arm teenagers with information about sex and pregnancy.

GUIDED READING QUESTIONS:

1. According to the viewpoint, how much money was spent on abstinence-until-married programs in 2006?
2. What falsehoods do abstinence-only education programs promote, according to the authors?
3. Name three public health groups that the authors say favor more comprehensive sex education programs.

F ederal funding for abstinence-unless-married education programs that often teach false, misleading, and inaccurate information received $178 million in FY 2006. Since 1996, over one billion in federal and state funding has been spent on these programs. As a result, these "just-say-no" programs, which promote abstinence from sexual activity as the sole message—without teaching basic facts about contraception and disease prevention—will continue to reach a growing number of children and adolescents.

The President's Budget for FY 2007 requests a total of $204 million for the three federally funded abstinence programs—a $28 million increase over last year. The drive to increase funding comes despite the mounting evidence that federally funded abstinence-unless-married education programs are not effective and at a time when programs that provide basic heath care services are struggling to keep up with the increasing demand for services. Instead, studies have shown that sex education that teaches about abstinence as well as contraception and disease prevention (comprehensive sex education) appears to be more effective in helping teens to delay sexual activity. . . .

Abstinence Programs Ignore Reality

Abstinence-unless-married programs ignore basic realities—that more than 60 percent of teenagers in the U.S. are sexually active before they finish high school.

- A total of 47% of teens in grades 9–12 are sexually active, however, teen sexual activity increases with age: 62% of teens in grade 12; 53% of teens in grade 11; 44% of teens in grade 10; and 33% of teens in grade 9, have had sex.
- Almost 850,000 teenagers become pregnant each year; more than one-third of teen girls become pregnant at least once before turning 20; and 78% of teenage pregnancies are unintended.
- Each year, 3 million teenagers contract a sexually transmitted disease; two-thirds of sexually transmitted infections occur in people under 25.
- Half of the 40,000 new cases of HIV infections each year occur to individuals under the age of 25—that means that an average of two young people is infected with HIV every hour of every day.

Federally funded abstinence-unless-married education curricula contain false, misleading, and distorted information intended to scare students rather than to educate. Despite the growing reliance on this

President George Bush sought increased funding for abstinence education, an approach that has supporters and detractors.

Misinformation about the effectiveness of condoms, which are prominently displayed in many drug stores, can be a problem.

approach to sex education, much of the information that America's youth are being taught is medically inaccurate or misleading, according to an analysis released by Congressman Henry Waxman (D-CA) on December 1, 2004. The report, which reviewed 13 curricula used by programs across the nation, confirms what advocates of comprehensive sex education have long argued—that many federally funded abstinence-unless-married education programs teach "false, misleading, or distorted information" about the risks of sexual activity.

Examples of misinformation contained in federally funded curricula:

- Condoms fail to prevent HIV transmission as often as 31 percent of the time in heterosexual intercourse.
- Touching a person's genitals can result in pregnancy; mutual masturbation can cause pregnancy.

- HIV can be transmitted by tears and sweat and fifty percent of gay teens have AIDS.
- A pregnancy occurs one out of every seven times that couples use condoms.
- A 43-day-old fetus is a "thinking person."
- Five to ten percent of women will never again be pregnant after having a legal abortion.
- Suicide is a consequence of premarital sex.

Since the Waxman report, the body of evidence showing that abstinence-only programs do not work has continued to grow.

A Record of Failure

State evaluations show little success in changing teens' behavior since the start of federal funding for abstinence programs.

- Advocates for Youth's analysis, Five Years of Abstinence-Only-Until-Marriage Education: Assessing the Impact, looked at evaluations from Arizona, Florida, Iowa, Maryland, Minnesota, Missouri, Nebraska, Oregon, Pennsylvania, and Washington state and found that abstinence-only programs show little evidence of sustained, long-term impact on adolescents' attitudes favoring abstinence or on teens' intentions to abstain. Importantly, in only one of the ten states did any program demonstrate short-term success in delaying the initiation of sex, and none showed long-term success in impacting teen sexual behavior.
- A January 2005 evaluation in Texas found that students in almost all high school grades were more sexually active after abstinence education. According to the study, about 23 percent of the ninth-grade girls in the study already had sexual intercourse before they received any abstinence education, a figure below the national average. After taking an abstinence course, the number among those same girls rose to 28 percent, a level closer to that of their peers across the state. Among ninth-grade boys, the percentage who reported sexual intercourse before and after abstinence education remained relatively unchanged. In 10th grade, however, the percentage of boys who had ever had sexual intercourse jumped from 24 percent to 39 percent after participating in an abstinence program.

- A review of programs in Ohio conducted by Case Western University School of Medicine found that participants in abstinence-only programs show no decrease in STD rates, are less likely to use a condom, and are more likely to engage in non-vaginal forms of intercourse, such as oral and anal sex. The report also found that these programs contain false or misleading information about contraceptives, abortion, and risks related to sexual activity.
- States have little say in how funds get spent, despite the Title V program's federal matching requirement of three state dollars for every four federal dollars. The restrictive definition led the state of California to turn down funding from the program's outset. Pennsylvania declined funding starting in FY 2004 based on the results of a state evaluation. Maine's Health and Human Services' Public Health Department announced in September 2005 that it would reject federal abstinence-only funds, becoming the third state to turn down these funds.

Mike Peters. Reproduced by permission.

Virginity Pledges Are Not the Answer

New research on virginity pledges from Yale University's Hannah Bruckner and Columbia University's Peter Bearman was published in the April 2005 issue of the Journal of Adolescent Health. Analyzing data from the National Longitudinal Study of Adolescent Health (Add Health) the researchers found that virginity pledge programs have had mixed results. They have been shown to delay intercourse up to 18 months, result in participating youth having fewer sex partners and getting married earlier. The long-term effectiveness of this approach, however, is questionable. The study analyzing the data found that 88% of pledgers had sex before marriage. In addition, teens who took pledges were just as likely to contract STDs as those who did not; the study found that this was because the virginity pledgers were less likely to use condoms when they did have sex.

Comprehensive Sex Ed Provides Kids with Tools

Comprehensive sex education can help delay sexual activity and give students the tools to avoid unintended pregnancy and STDs when they do become sexually active. Research done by Douglas Kirby for the National Campaign to Prevent Teen Pregnancy shows that programs that provide teenagers with comprehensive sex education that includes a discussion of contraception in addition to abstinence can be effective in helping teens to delay sexual activity, to use contraceptives when they do become sexually active, and to have fewer partners. In contrast, abstinence-only messages have been shown to reduce contraceptive use among sexually active teens, putting them at risk of pregnancy and STDs, including HIV.

Contraception is responsible for half of the recent decline in teen pregnancy. An August 2004 report from the Centers for Disease Control and Prevention (CDC) attributes 53 percent of the decrease in teen pregnancy to increased abstinence and 47 percent to increased use of contraceptives.

Major medical, public health research groups and institutions support more comprehensive forms of sex education that includes information about both abstinence and contraception. They include the American Medical Association, the American Academy of Pediatrics, the American Nurses Association, the American College of Obstetricians and Gynecologists, the American Psychological Association, the American Public Health Association, the National Institutes of Health, and the Institute of Medicine.

Americans support more comprehensive forms of sex education, reflecting the minimal public support for abstinence-unless-married agendas that reflects political rather than public health concerns. A January 2004 poll from NPR/Kaiser Family Foundation/Harvard Kennedy School of Government showed that a majority of parents want abstinence to be a major piece of a sex education curriculum. However, only 15 percent of parents believed that schools should teach only about abstinence from sexual intercourse and should not provide information on condoms and contraception.

EVALUATING THE AUTHOR'S ARGUMENTS:

The author of this viewpoint argues that abstinence-only education does not work because teenagers are going to have sex despite messages to abstain. Daniel Allott, the author of the previous viewpoint, however, argues that it is wrong to assume that teens are necessarily going to have premarital sex. What do you think? Is it right or wrong to assume that teenagers are inevitably going to have sex?

Teaching About Contraception Can Reduce Teen Pregnancy

"Do we want sexually active youth not to use condoms? I don't think so."

Advocates for Youth

The following viewpoint is an excerpt from a speech delivered by a youth activist named Jennifer at a national conference on sexual health. Jennifer is a member of Advocates for Youth, an organization that works to promote sex education that teaches teens about both contraception and abstinence. In the speech, Jennifer argues that much of current sex education does not tell teenagers the truth about the effectiveness and use of contraception. This deception must stop, she states, because it causes teenagers to not trust adults and also causes them to have unsafe sexual experiences. We must speak honestly to teens about their sexual health, Jennifer says, and that includes teaching them about contraception. She concludes that when teenagers

Jennifer, Activist and Educator, "Common Sense: America's Youth and Sexual Health," *www.advocatesfor youth.org*, May 25, 2004. Reproduced by permission.

know how to use condoms and other forms of birth control, teen pregnancy rates will go down.

GUIDED READING QUESTIONS:
1. What lie was one girl living in a low-income community told about condoms?
2. According to Jennifer, what does adult discomfort with teen sexuality lead to?
3. What does *ABC* in the "ABC approach" stand for?

I think it is important to establish the difference between children and young people. What may sound like semantics is actually an important distinction, since sexual health policy aimed towards "children" oftentimes overlooks that these "children" quickly become autonomous adults. Young people easily recognize, and just as easily dismiss, paternalistic, condescending approaches. Young people need to feel that they are respected as thinking, competent human beings, primarily because, and Read My Lips: *YOUNG PEOPLE ARE CAPABLE OF MAKING EDUCATED DECISIONS ABOUT THEIR SEXUAL HEALTH OF THEIR OWN VOLITION.* However, this comes at a price—educated decisions cannot be made on the basis of false information. Accurate, honest facts are necessary, by definition, for responsible, educated decision-making.

FAST FACT

According to SIECUS, 93 percent of parents of high school students believe that birth control and other methods of pregnancy prevention are appropriate topics for education programs in schools.

Sex Education Inaccurate

It's hardly surprising that America's current scare tactic approaches aren't working. Young people are not stupid. Believe me, I know. They also don't appreciate being manipulated, which in fact they are, when the information they are given is itself manipulated. And most importantly, if people, young or old, feel that they are being manipulated, they lose the ability to trust. This we *all* know! If we can't trust an information source and, by extension, the information itself, then we're likely to disregard both. By scare tactics, I mean the misinformation incorporated into many sex education curricula—misinformation that is meant to cause paralyzing fear, enforcing abstinence. A girl living in a low-income community area on the south side of Chicago told me that her sex education teacher in her public school told her condoms had holes in them. So we tell young people that condoms have holes in them! This is a gross exaggeration whose effects are far-reaching and unilaterally damaging. What is the purpose of providing this false information? Do we want sexually active youth not to use condoms? I don't think so. . . .

Contraception Is an Important Tool Kids Need

The goal is not to impose a particular lifestyle on a young person. The goal is to empower young people to make healthy decisions of their own accord, not only in the classroom but also in the realities of life.

Students pause to listen to a classmate. Inaccurate information can make it even more difficult for teens to make good decisions.

Teens who are sexually active can benefit from information about birth control pills (pictured) and other methods of contraception.

While some young people will decide to abstain from all types of sex, most will not. AND THERE IS NOTHING WRONG WITH THIS. Young people, just like all other people, are sexual beings. I understand that this may be a hard concept to be comfortable with. It is difficult. Yet it is essential that our parents, guardians, teachers, doctors and everyone else who cares about our development realize that we are human. And as humans, we are sexual. Adult discomfort with this fact is dangerous—it leads to willful ignorance—ignorance such as thinking that telling a girl that condoms have holes in them will make her never have sex before marriage. It is possible. But it's also possible that she will engage in some type of sexual activity before marriage, and isn't it better for everyone to be honest and realistic—so that real communication can take place. And she can make responsible decisions.

It is the responsibility of the positive adult role models who are involved in youth's development to feel comfortable with sexuality as normal. Sex does not have to be a problem-oriented subject; there are many aspects of sex and sexuality that have little to do with HIV/AIDS, teen pregnancy, or sexually transmitted infections. SEX IS GOOD! Discussing sex only in the context of danger is psychologically damaging, since we are all sexual beings. Should we always be afraid and feel guilty when we think and talk about sex? No. We should be well informed and, therefore, confident of our decisions. I understand the level of discomfort that is inherent in these conversations, discomfort that reflects a certain shame or embarrassment that our society has around sex; however, it is time to get over it. I have found over and over again that, the more comfortable I am talking about a particular subject, the more comfortable the young people I am talking to become. . . .

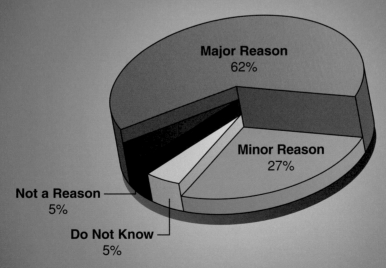

Education and Teen Pregnancy

A 2004 poll found that the majority of parents believed that including contraception in sex education programs was responsible for a drop in teen pregnancy rates.

Major Reason
62%

Minor Reason
27%

Not a Reason
5%

Do Not Know
5%

*Numbers do not add up to 100 because 1% of respondents refused to answer.

Source: National Public Radio/Kaiser Family Foundation/Kennedy School of Government, January 2004.

We Must Teach About Contraception

So, you may ask, aside from attitudinal changes to promote honesty and respect, what, specifically, do I think needs to be done? What should we teach youth? In my opinion, I think the *ABC approach* that is being taken in Uganda could work well in the United States. However, it can only work if the slogan of Abstinence, Be Faithful and use Condoms is kept in tact. Its integrity is in its comprehensive approach to sexual activity. I particularly like this approach because it does not make value judgments on any of the sub-parts. I also like the ABC approach because, if applied properly, it respects the decision making abilities of young people. Each of the options, whether it be abstinence or faithfulness or condom use, is appropriate for different people at different times in their lives. And this strategy allows room for individuals, all individuals, young or old, to make choices that are appropriate for them. Some might say that the ABC approach or something similar has already been tried in the United States and has not worked. This, I can say from personal experience as a high school student in Virginia and a health educator in Illinois, is not true. Honest, *comprehensive sex education* has not been supported in the United States yet. . . .

I hope some of what I have said today will shed greater light on the issues that are on the table. While they are complex and often emotionally loaded, I do believe in common ground. I have seen it and heard it here today. But more importantly, I have to believe in common ground for the sake of myself, my peers and our future.

EVALUATING THE AUTHOR'S ARGUMENTS:

Jennifer, the author of the above viewpoint that argues in favor of teaching contraception, is a teenager herself. The author of the next viewpoint you will read, who argues against teaching contraception, is an adult. Do their ages give one author more authority to speak on the subject of teen sex than the other? Give your reasons.

Teaching About Contraception Is Wrong

Rebecca Hagelin

"Contraception is discussed ad nauseam. . . . [It's] not exactly the message most parents want presented to their judgment-impaired teens."

The author of the following viewpoint, Rebecca Hagelin, is the vice president of the Heritage Foundation, a conservative think tank. In this article she argues that much of the sex education in schools includes far too much discussion of contraception and premarital sex. Hagelin writes that these discussions are immoral, and she entreats parents to put an end to this type of sex education. Students should not be taught that teen sex is normal and should not learn about how to find and use condoms. These programs, states Hagelin, push children unnecessarily towards sexual activity.

GUIDED READING QUESTIONS:
1. What activities take place in sex education classes, according to the author?
2. What do the sex education programs discussed by the author say about homosexuality?
3. What percentage of parents said that teens should wait until they have finished high school to have sex?

Rebecca Hagelin, "Parents Beware," *www.heritage.org*, February 11, 2005. Reproduced by permission.

arents, does the school your children attend feature a sex-education program that's billed as "abstinence-based" or "abstinence-plus"? If so, you may be under the understandable impression that it tells teens, in clear-cut language, that they're not ready for sex. That they should wait. That it focuses on . . . well, abstinence.

But a major study from The Heritage Foundation, "*Comprehensive Sex Education vs. Authentic Abstinence: A Study of Competing Curricula,*" shows that isn't the case. Like "People for the American Way" or "Planned Parenthood," the label "abstinence-plus" is a flat-out lie. There's a lot of "plus" and precious little "abstinence."

Pushing Condoms on Kids

Contraception is discussed ad nauseam. "Condoms are available at any drugstore or family planning clinic," teens are told in one program, absurdly titled *Reducing the Risk*. "They may also be available in outdoor or all-night condom vending machines. Anyone can buy condoms, regardless of age, and no prescription is needed." Not exactly the message most parents want presented to their judgment-impaired teens. Yet, as the Heritage study shows, such messages are commonplace in "comprehensive" sex-ed programs.

Worse, the programs often rely on role-playing games that are plainly designed to reinforce immoral behavior and break down the natural modesty that might otherwise keep many teens from engaging in pre-marital sex. In *Becoming a Responsible Teen* (another eye-rolling misnomer), students are given the following scenario: "My partner and I are alone. We've been leading up to sex for a couple of weeks. The only thing we haven't discussed is protection. My partner needs to persuade me to use a latex condom."

Well, this parent has a different suggestion: Things shouldn't even get this far, but if they do, one of the kids needs to say a firm no. When will that be taught?

Not surprisingly, some of these programs also present homosexuality as just another "lifestyle choice" that's above reproach. In

FAST FACT

In 1913 the Chicago public school system became the first in the nation to teach sex education.

Some critics of sex education in schools argue that programs do not put enough emphasis on abstinence.

Be Proud! Be Responsible!, teens are told, "You can accept your bisexuality." In *Reducing the Risk*, we find this role-playing exercise: "Tony and Dylan have been to a party and then go to Tony's home to be alone. They start to kiss and undress each other. Dylan reaches into his jacket pocket and realizes that he doesn't have the condom he planned to use. . . . What can Tony and Dylan do to avoid unprotected sex?"

These Programs Are Lewd and Disgusting

And that's the tame stuff. From condom "races" (seeing which team of students can be the first to successfully unroll one onto a banana or a cucumber) to graphic descriptions of how teens can perform oral sex on each other "safely," these programs are frequently lewd and disgusting. I lack the space (and the stomach, quite frankly) to cite every example, so I'll refer the terminally curious to the Heritage report mentioned earlier.

The underlying message is unmistakable: Teen sex is normal, so let's just tell the kids how to avoid pregnancy and disease. There's a token nod or two to abstinence, but as Heritage's Robert Rector notes, it often amounts to a sentence or two amid pages and pages of explicit, pro-condom propaganda. Teens get the impression that abstinence is some unattainable ideal—not the only option that's fail safe (not to mention moral).

Parents, peers, and school programs all play a part in decisions teens make about sex and relationships, although some of these influences are positive and some are not.

You probably need little proof that parents want such pornography kept far from their kids, but a Zogby International poll of more than 1,000 parents of school-age children provides some: 91 percent said they want teens taught that "sex should be linked to love, intimacy and commitment, and that these qualities are most likely to occur in marriage." In overwhelming numbers, they rejected the morally objectionable content and approach of "abstinence-plus" programs.

Asked when sexual activity should begin, more than three out of every four parents said teens should wait until they're married or close to marriage. Another 12 percent said to wait until they've at least finished high school. Only 7 percent said "protected sex" in high school is OK. Yet that's almost exclusively what these programs teach our teens.

Parents Must Insist on Abstinence-Only Education

Which means that we're setting them up for failure. A host of social-science research shows that *early sexual activity is dangerous* not just because of sexually transmitted diseases, but because it hampers the ability to form stable marriages later in life (making the additional $38 million President Bush has proposed for abstinence-only programs a sound investment).

Parents, your teens deserve an unambiguous abstinence message. If your school isn't providing one, you need to equip yourself with *reliable research*, network with other parents and make a change. It's time to subtract the "plus" from "abstinence-plus."

EVALUATING THE AUTHOR'S ARGUMENTS:

The author of this viewpoint, Rebecca Hagelin, believes that teens should not be taught about contraception in their sex education classes. The author of the preceding viewpoint, Jennifer, states that teens deserve to know about contraception. If you were in a debate, which author would you side with? Why?

Glossary

abortifacient: Most often, a drug or other chemical substance that causes abortion in a pregnant woman.

abortion: A medical procedure in which a fetus or embryo is removed from the mother's uterus.

abstinence: The practice of refraining entirely from an act, such as sex.

abstinence-only sex education: The name given to sex education programs that promote refraining from sex until marriage and do not provide information on contraception or abortion.

Ayotte v. Planned Parenthood of Northern New England: The January 2006 U.S. Supreme Court decision stating that abortion laws must protect pregnant women's health and safety. The case was spurred by the passage of a New Hampshire law that required doctors to notify a pregnant teenager's parents before performing an abortion, with no provision for the health of the teenager.

comprehensive sex education: The name given to sex education programs, most often in public schools, that seek to include all aspects of sexuality concerns, including information on contraception, abstinence, abortion, and sexually transmitted diseases. Also called "abstinence-plus."

contraception: The prevention of pregnancy through various methods that may include drugs, barriers such as condoms or diaphragms, sexual practices such as withdrawal, or medical procedures.

emergency contraception: Refers to a type of drug with a high dose of hormones that can be taken after unprotected sex to prevent pregnancy. Also called the morning-after pill.

partial-birth abortion: A controversial term used to describe late-term abortions.

premarital sex: Sex before marriage.

pro-choice: A term used to describe someone who believes abortion should be legal and women should be allowed to decide for themselves if they want to abort a pregnancy.

pro-life: A term used to describe someone who believes abortion is immoral and should be illegal.

virginity pledge: Refers to a public promise made mostly by teenagers, especially among some Christian denominations, to refrain from sex until marriage.

Facts About Teen Pregnancy

Editor's note: These facts can be used in reports or papers to reinforce or add credibility when making important points or claims.

Teen Pregnancy Around the World
- According to the sexuality education group Advocates for Youth, teenagers in Europe have sex at about the same rate as American teenagers, yet Europeans have a far lower rate of teen pregnancy.
- BBC News reported in 2005 that Britain had the highest teen pregnancy rate in Europe.
- In some developing nations, such as Bangladesh, Niger, Nepal, and the Philippines, girls are frequently married and have children by the time they are fourteen.
- In parts of western Africa, 40 percent of girls between fifteen and nineteen are married, according to the United Nations.

Teen Pregnancy in the United States
- According to the Centers for Disease Control and Prevention, Washington, D.C., has the highest teen birthrate in the country at eighty-one births per one thousand teens, and 47 percent of U.S. high school students say they have had sex at least once during high school.
- The Kaiser Family Foundation reported in 2005 that one-third of U.S. girls will become pregnant before they turn twenty, and 80 percent of those will be unmarried.
- According the National Campaign to Prevent Teen Pregnancy, teen pregnancy rates are higher in the southern and western regions of the United States.
- During the 1950s many girls married before turning nineteen, but by the late 1970s the average age for marriage had risen to twenty-three, states historian Jeffrey P. Moran in his book *Teaching Sex*.

- A 1990 study by the Brookings Institution showed that almost one-half of all teenage mothers began receiving welfare within five years of having a baby.

According to the National Abortion Federation:
- Each year, one million American teenagers become pregnant.
- 78 percent of these pregnancies are unwanted.
- About 35 percent of teenage girls who become pregnant choose to have an abortion rather than deliver a child.

Teen Pregnancy and Race, Gender, and Ethnicity
- According to the Department of Health and Human Services, 14 percent of teenage boys who have had sex say that they have also caused a pregnancy.
- The *New York Times* reported in 2004 that 65 percent of sexually active high school boys said they used condoms regularly.
- Nationally, black women have abortions at nearly three times the rate of white women, according to the Centers for Disease Control and Prevention.
- In Mississippi, black women accounted for 72 percent of the state's abortions in 2002, according to U.S. census data.
- A study conducted by Motivational Educational Entertainment in 2004 found that black adolescents are becoming sexually active at younger ages than other youth.

According to a February 2005 report by the research organization Child Trends:
- In general, Hispanic teens have a higher rate of pregnancy than the overall U.S. population.
- Among Hispanic teens, those of Mexican origin have the highest rate of birth, and those of Cuban origin have the lowest rate.
- One-quarter of all Hispanic women will give birth before the age of twenty.
- Pregnant Hispanic teens are more likely to marry the father of their baby than teens from other racial and ethnic groups.

According to an analysis released by the National Campaign to Prevent Teen Pregnancy in May 2006:

- Almost one-third of all sexually experienced teen girls have been pregnant.
- More than one in eight sexually experienced teen boys have caused a pregnancy.
- Teen girls who first have sex before the age of fifteen are significantly more likely to become pregnant than those who have sex after the age of fifteen.
- Teens who use contraception the first time they have sex are less likely to report being involved in a pregnancy than those who do not.

Organizations to Contact

Advocates for Youth
2000 M St. NW, Suite 750
Washington, DC 20036
(202) 419-3420
e-mail: information@advocatesforyouth.org
Web site: www.advocatesforyouth.org

Formerly the Center for Population Options, Advocates for Youth is the only national organization focusing solely on pregnancy and HIV prevention among young people. It provides information, education, and advocacy to youth-serving agencies and professionals, policy makers, and the media.

Alan Guttmacher Institute
120 Wall St.
New York, NY 10005
(212) 248-1111
e-mail: info@guttmacher.org
Web site: www.alanguttmacher.org

The institute works to protect people's access to the information and services they need to make decisions about sexual activity, reproduction, and family planning. Among the institute's publications are the books *Teenage Pregnancy in Industrialized Countries* and *Today's Adolescents, Tomorrow's Parents: A Portrait of the Americas* and the report "Sex and America's Teenagers."

Campaign for Our Children (CFOC)
1 N. Charles St., Suite 1100
Baltimore, MD 21201
(410) 576-9015
Web site: www.cfoc.org

The CFOC is a nonprofit organization that works to address the high teen pregnancy rate in Maryland and also across the nation. The CFOC focuses on educating teenagers to lower the teen pregnancy rate.

Child Trends, Inc. (CT)
4301 Connecticut Ave. NW, Suite 100
Washington, DC 20008
(202) 572-6000
Web site: www.childtrends.org

CT works to provide accurate statistical and research information regarding children and their families in the United States and to educate the American public on the ways existing social trends—such as the increasing rate of teenage pregnancy—affect children.

Concerned Women for America (CWA)
1015 15th St. NW, Suite 1100
Washington, DC 20005
(202) 488-7000
Web site: www.cwfa.org

CWA's purpose is to preserve, protect, and promote traditional Judeo-Christian values through education, legislative action, and other activities. CWA publishes the monthly *Family Voice*, which periodically addresses issues such as abortion and promoting sexual abstinence in schools.

Family Research Council
801 G St. NW
Washington, DC 20001
(202) 393-2100
Web site: www.frc.org

The council seeks to promote and protect the interests of the traditional family. It focuses on issues such as parental autonomy and responsibility, community support for single parents, and adolescent pregnancy. Among the council's numerous publications are the papers "Revolt of the Virgins," "Abstinence: The New Sexual Revolution," and "Abstinence Programs Show Promise in Reducing Sexual Activity and Pregnancy Among Teens."

Focus on the Family
8605 Explorer Dr.
Colorado Springs, CO 80920

(719) 531-3400
Web site: www.family.org

Focus on the Family is a Christian organization dedicated to preserving and strengthening the traditional family. It believes that the breakdown of the traditional family is in part linked to increases in teen pregnancy, and so it conducts research on the ethics of condom use and the effectiveness of safe-sex education programs in schools.

Healthy Teen Network
509 Second St. NE
Washington, DC 20002
(202) 547-8814
Web site: www.healthyteennetwork.org

The Healthy Teen Network, formerly the National Organization of Adolescent Pregnancy, Parenting, and Prevention, promotes comprehensive and coordinated services designed for the prevention and resolution of problems associated with adolescent pregnancy and parenthood. The organization publishes the *Prevention Researcher*, a quarterly journal and various fact sheets on teen pregnancy.

Heritage Foundation
214 Massachusetts Ave. NE
Washington, DC 20002
(202) 546-4400
e-mail: info@heritage.org
Web site: www.heritage.org

The Heritage Foundation is a public policy research institute that believes the welfare system has contributed to the problems of illegitimacy and teenage pregnancy. Among the foundation's numerous publications is its Backgrounder series, which includes "Liberal Welfare Programs: What the Data Show on Programs for Teenage Mothers"; the paper "Rising Illegitimacy: America's Social Catastrophe"; and the bulletin "How Congress Can Protect the Rights of Parents to Raise Their Children."

National Abortion and Reproductive Rights Action League (NARAL Pro-Choice America)
1156 15th St. NW, Suite 700

Washington, DC 20005
(272) 973-3000
Web site: www.prochoiceamerica.org

The goal of NARAL, which has groups in more than forty states, is to develop and sustain a pro-choice political constituency in order to maintain the right of all women to legal abortion.

National Campaign to Prevent Teen Pregnancy
1776 Massachusetts Ave. NW, Suite 200
Washington, DC 20036
(202) 478-8500
e-mail: campaign@teenpregnancy.org
Web site: www.teenpregnancy.org

The goal of the National Campaign to Prevent Teen Pregnancy is to prevent teen pregnancy by supporting values and stimulating actions that are consistent with a pregnancy-free adolescence. The organization publishes the report "Whatever Happened to Childhood? The Problem of Teen Pregnancy in the United States."

Planned Parenthood Federation of America (PPFA)
434 W. 33rd St.
New York, NY 10001
(212) 541-7800
e-mail: communications@ppfa.org
Web site: www.plannedparenthood.org

The PPFA is a national organization that supports people's right to make their own reproductive decisions without governmental interference. In 1989 it developed First Things First, a nationwide adolescent pregnancy prevention program. Among the PPFA's numerous publications are the booklets *Teen Sex?*, *Facts About Birth Control*, and *How to Talk with Your Teen About the Facts of Life.*

Sexuality Information and Education Council of the United States (SIECUS)
130 W. 42nd St., Suite 350
New York, NY 10036
(212) 819-9770

e-mail: siecus@siecus.org

Web site: www.siecus.org

SIECUS promotes comprehensive education about sexuality and advocates the right of individuals to make responsible sexual choices. In addition to providing guidelines for sexuality education for kindergarten through twelfth grade, SIECUS publishes the reports "Facing Facts: Sexual Health for America's Adolescents" and "Teens Talk About Sex: Adolescent Sexuality in the 90s" and the fact sheet "Adolescents and Abstinence."

For Further Reading

Books

Bachiochi, Erika, *The Cost of "Choice": Women Evaluate the Impact of Abortion*. New York: Encounter, 2007. A book offering a pro-life view of abortion.

Baird, Robert M. and Stuart E. Rosenbaum, *The Ethics of Abortion: Pro-Life vs. Pro-Choice*. Amherst, NY: Prometheus, 2001. The authors of this young-adult book present a balanced view of different arguments on abortion.

Cherry, Andrew L., *Teenage Pregnancy: A Global View*. Westport, CT: Greenwood, 2001. This reference book discusses the issue of teen pregnancy around the world.

Coles, Robert, *The Youngest Parents: Teenage Pregnancy as It Shapes Lives*. New York: W.W. Norton, 2000. Written by a psychiatrist, this book offers a glimpse into the daily lives of teen parents.

Davis, Deborah, *You Look Too Young to Be a Mom: Teen Mothers on Love, Learning, and Success*. New York: Perigee, 2004. This book tells the stories of thirty teen mothers and how they experienced their pregnancies and their lives afterward.

Ehrlich, J. Shoshanna, *Who Decides? The Abortion Rights of Teens*. Westport, CT: Praeger, 2006. A law professor discusses the issue of parental and judicial involvement in teen abortion.

Englander, Annrenee and Corinne Wilks, *Dear Diary, I'm Pregnant: Teenagers Talk About Their Pregnancy*. Ontario: Annick, 1997. A compilation of ten monologues from pregnant teens, recording their thoughts and feelings.

Knowles, Jon, *All About Birth Control: A Complete Guide*. New York: Three Rivers, 1998. This practical sourcebook presents a comprehensive list of types of available birth control methods, effectiveness, and side effects.

Lerman, Evelyn, *Teen Moms: The Pain and the Promise*. Buena Park, CA: Morning Glory, 1997. This book provides general factual background on teen pregnancy, including research results and statistics.

Luker, Kristin, *Dubious Conceptions: The Politics of Teenage Pregnancy.* Cambridge, MA: Harvard University Press, 1997. This scholarly text focuses on the causes of teenage pregnancy, using the problem to reflect on American society as a whole.

Luttrell, Wendy, *Pregnant Bodies, Fertile Minds: Gender, Race, and the Schooling of Pregnant Teens.* New York: Routledge, 2002. Written by a professor of education, this book presents the results of a study of a program for pregnant teens.

Pillow, Wanda S., *Unfit Subjects: Education Policy and the Teen Mother, 1972–2002.* New York: Routledge, 2003. Analyzes government policies with regards to the education of teenage mothers, using scholarly theories as background.

South Vista Education Center, *Daycare and Diplomas: Teen Mothers Who Stayed in School.* Minneapolis, MN: Fairview Press, 2001. A short book for young readers containing essays by young women who have been both mothers and students.

Periodicals

Allott, Daniel, "The Abortion Effect," *American Spectator*, January 24, 2006.

Bernstein, Nina, "Behind Fall in Pregnancy, a New Teenage Culture of Restraint," *New York Times*, March 7, 2004.

Britt, Donna, "In Another Era, Teen Mom Was a Cautionary Tale," *Washington Post*, April 15, 2005.

Broussard, Sharon, "Teen Pregnancy: Private Act, Public Concern," *Cleveland (OH) Plain Dealer*, April 4, 2004.

Bussel, Rachel Kramer, "Teens' Sexual Rights," *Village Voice*, April 13, 2005.

Cramer, Elisa, "Is It Sex if You Can't Get Pregnant?" *Palm Beach Post*, April 16, 2004.

Dalven, Jennifer, "Is New Hampshire's Parental Abortion Act Constitutional?" *Supreme Court Debates*, January 2006.

Davis, Thulani, "The Height of Disrespect," *Village Voice*, March 23, 2004.

De Solenni Pia, "The Mourning After," *American Spectator*, September 8, 2005.

Feagans, Brian, "Latinos Re-examine Pregnancy in Teens," *Atlanta Journal-Constitution*, October 12, 2005.

Feldman, Sally, "Why I'm Glad My Daughter Had Underage Sex," *Humanist*, November 1, 2004.

Forsythe, Clarke D., "Supreme Opportunity," *National Review*, November 30, 2005.

Gonzalez, Maria Cortes, "Young Love," *El Paso Times*, February 13, 2006.

Haddock, Vicki, "Key to Sex Education: Discipline or Knowledge," *San Francisco Chronicle*, May 22, 2005.

Heartfield, Kate, "Knowledge Makes Teen Sexuality Safer," *Ottawa Citizen*, November 2, 2004.

Hillman, Diane I., "What Do You Do After She Says, 'I'm Pregnant?'" *Adoptive Families Association of Tompkins County Newsletter*, August 4, 2004.

Hoder, Randye, "Sex Education for Parents, Too," *Los Angeles Times*, February 13, 2006.

Jayson, Sharon, "Teens Define Sex in New Ways," *USA Today*, October 19, 2005.

Jossi, Frank, "Sharp Decline in Teen Pregnancy Prompts Researchers to Ponder What Works," *Contemporary Sexuality*, September 2005.

Juarez, Vanessa, "Talking to Teenagers About. . .," *Newsweek*, November 21, 2005.

McKay, Betsy and Ann Carrns, "As Teen Births Drop, Experts Are Asking Why," *Wall Street Journal*, November 17, 2004.

Malin, Joan, "Why We Care," *New York Amsterdam News*, December 15, 2005.

Morford, Mark, "Sex and the Disgruntled Teen," *San Francisco Chronicle*, Februrary 25, 2005.

Page, Clarence, "Teach Children to Respect Themselves," *Seattle Post-Intelligencer*, March 25, 2004.

Pinkerton, James, "Keeping Mom in Class," *Houston Chronicle*, March 21, 2004.

Rinehart, Diane, "Girls Gone Awry," *Vancouver Sun*, September 30, 2005.

Rosen, Jeffrey, "The Day After Roe," *Atlantic Monthly*, June 2006.

Sanders, Joshua, "Teen Sex Report Paints Grim Picture," *San Francisco Chronicle*, April 4, 2004.

Schiffrin, Reina and Joann D. Smith, "Don't Let Abortion Foes Chip Away at Roe," *Newsday*, December 1, 2005.

Shah, Allie, "Sex and the Ring," *Minneapolis (MN) Star Tribune*, September 11, 2005.

Skipp, Catharine, "The Case of L.G.," *Newsweek*, April 29, 2005.

Vincent, Lynn, "Healthy Skepticism," *World Magazine*, June 19, 2004.

Wisdom, D. Linsey, "Passion Not Worth a Teen Pregnancy," *Atlanta Journal-Constitution*, October 5, 2005.

Internet Sources

Baker, Linda, "A Teen Mom Reaches High," January 16, 2006. www.connectforkids.org.

Brown, Sarah, "What Should Young People Be Taught in Sex Education?" February 8, 2005. www.teenpregnancy.org.

Grogan, Kaye, "Maybe It's Time for Separation of School and Sex?" March 16, 2006. www.towhhall.com.

Pardue, Melissa G., "More Evidence of the Effectiveness of Abstinence Education Programs," May 5, 2005. www.heritage.org.

Rector, Robert E., "Facts About Abstinence Education," March 30, 2004. www.heritage.org.

Weyrich, Paul, "Abstinence Education Works," February 15, 2005. www.renewamerica.us.

Yudt, Susan, "Why Teens Need Emergency Contraception," May 21, 2004. www.teenwire.com.

Web Sites

Connect for Kids (www.connectforkids.org). A national nonprofit organization that uses the Internet to provide information about kids to parents and guardians. The Web site provides information on adoption, foster care, public assistance, and teen motherhood.

March of Dimes (www.marchofdimes.com). This nonprofit organization is dedicated to improving the health of babies through public education and advocacy. Its Web site maintains extensive information on issues often affecting the babies of teenagers, such as low birth weight and premature birth.

TeenBreaks.com (www.teenbreaks.com). A teen-support Web site run by the Rosetta Foundation, an organization that supports pro-life values. It offers testimonials by teens who are or have been pregnant as well as advice on options other than abortion.

Teen Mother Choices (www.teenmotherchoices.org). This Christian-based group exists to discourage pregnant teens from choosing abortion and to support them through their pregnancies. The Web site offers adoption advice and support for those who keep their babies.

Teen Wire (www.teenwire.com). A sexual health Web site specifically for teens, run by Planned Parenthood of America. It includes articles written by teens about sex, answers to commonly asked questions, and information on pregnancy and sexually transmitted diseases.

Index

Picture Credits

Cover: © David Young-Wolff/Photo Edit
© A.J. Sisco/CORBIS, 91
© David Young-Wolff/Photo Edit, 13
DK Stock/Getty Images, 106
© Estelle Klawitter/zefa/CORBIS, 85
Getty Images, 21, 39, 40
© Greg Smith/CORBIS, 12
© Jed Share/CORBIS, 78
© Kate Mitchell/zefa/CORBIS, 50
© Laura Dwight/Photo Edit, 67
© LWA-Dann Tardif/CORBIS, 69, 99
© Mark Richards/Photo Edit, 61
© Mary Kate Denny/Photo Edit, 65
© Pete Leonard/zefa/CORBIS, 47
PhotoDisc, 60, 77
Photolibrary.com/Jupiter Images, 37
Photonica/Getty Images 30, 100
Photos.com, 22, 24, 74, 87
© Rick Gomez/CORBIS, 48
Rick Steele/UPI/Landov, 15
© ROB & SAS/CORBIS, 35
© Robert Brenner/Photo Edit, 64
© SGO/Image Point FR/CORBIS, 55
Steve Zmina, 16, 42, 56, 72, 86, 101
Stone/Getty Images 28, 105
Taxi/Getty Images, 10
The Image Bank/Getty Images, 53, 73
Time & Life Pictures/Getty Images, 92

About the Editor

Emma Carlson Berne holds a master's degree in composition-rhetoric from Miami University in Oxford, Ohio. She has written and edited many books for middle and high-school students, including *Introducing Issues with Opposing Viewpoints: Abortion* and a biography of the rapper Snoop Dogg. Emma lives in Charleston, South Carolina, with her husband Aaron.